RESEARCH

How to Plan, Speak and Write About It

Edited by
Clifford Hawkins and Marco Sorgi

Foreword by Stephen Lock

With 55 Figures

Springer-Verlag
Berlin Heidelberg New York Tokyo
1985

Clifford Hawkins, MD, FRCP
Honorary Consultant Physician, Queen Elizabeth Hospital,
Birmingham and Senior Clinical Lecturer to the University of
Birmingham, England

Marco Sorgi, MD, MASVS
Consultant Surgeon to the Venezuelan Health Service; Senior
Lecturer (Ad Honorem), School of Medicine, Caracas,
Venezuela

ISBN 3-540-13992-3 Springer-Verlag Berlin Heidelberg New York Tokyo
ISBN 0-387-13992-3 Springer-Verlag New York Heidelberg Berlin Tokyo

Library of Congress Cataloging in Publication Data
Main entry under title:
Research: how to plan, speak and write about it. Bibliography: p. Includes
index. 1. Research. 2. Medicine – Research. I. Hawkins, Clifford F. II. Sorgi.
Marco. Q180.A1R444   1985   001.4   85-2656
ISBN 0-387-13992-3 (U.S.)

The use of general descriptive names, trade marks, etc. in this publication,
even if the former are not especially identified, is not relevant to be taken as
a sign that such names, as understood by the Trade Marks and Merchandise
Marks Act, may accordingly be used freely by anyone.

Filmset by Wenden Typesetting Services Limited, Wenden Court,
Wendens Ambo, Saffron Walden, Essex.
Printed by R. J. Acford, Terminus Road Industrial Estate, Chichester,
Sussex.

2128/3916–54321

Preface

Training for research is only available in a few places in the world, so that usually the researcher has to learn to master every step by himself. This entails planning the research, finding out how to obtain funds, searching the literature, analysing the data statistically, preparing visual material and slides, speaking about it in public, writing it up for journals and so on.

Books on various aspects of this subject are readily obtainable but this is an attempt to deal with all the steps that are necessary from the start to the finish, and chapters have been planned sequentially with this in mind. Although most of the authors are doctors of medicine, it should help those in any area of science where the undertaking and publishing of research is important.

Marco Sorgi conceived the idea of the book and, during an appointment in the University of Birmingham, invited Clifford Hawkins to help in achieving its delivery. May the effort be found to be worthwhile.

Birmingham, England 1984   Clifford Hawkins
                                            Marco Sorgi

Acknowledgements

We thank Miss Karen Roberts who typed the manuscript on the word processor and patiently dealt with all the revisions. Mr Paul Busby drew the cartoons and Mr Derek Virtue put his professional touch to the line diagrams. Michael Jackson, Medical Editor at Springer, has been of immense help throughout.

Foreword

Few would disagree with the proposition that research is incomplete until its results have been communicated. Preferably this is best done in print, where the background to the study, the details of the methods, the data in extenso, the placing of new findings in the perspective of the old, and the formulation of a new hypothesis can all be exposed to the critical reader and enshrined in permanent form. So, not surprisingly, the eminent physicist and science philosopher, Professor John Ziman, has declared that, "The object of research is publication".

Nevertheless, like patriotism, publication is still not enough: an article has to be read. Every peer reviewer, or referee, knows how many articles are almost unintelligible in their unpublished form. And even after these have been revised, subedited, and printed, citation analysis tells us that between a third and a half of them are never cited even once in subsequent reference lists, leading some of us to suspect that many articles are hardly read at all.

If death by neglect is not to be the fate of many scientific articles what can be done about it? One of the main reasons for this neglect, I suspect, is the poor quality of the articles, which lack a logical structure and are written in contorted language. Nevertheless, we should not blame the scientist: he has not been taught good scientific writing and he will be unlikely to gather what this is from looking at most published articles. He needs to be taught — by ad hominem discussions with his colleagues, by short courses, and by books. All of these have complementary roles, but for the person who is isolated (not necessarily by geography) the last, with its permanent qualities, may be the most important. We should never forget, moreover, that communication means more than the written word, that speaking about research is often as poorly done as writing about it, and that using a few rules about speaking will transform a verbal presentation as effectively as using those about writing will transform the printed account.

For all these reasons, therefore, I welcome the initiative by the Editors in bringing together a team of experts to discuss better communication in all its forms. Action on their recommendations would mean fewer headaches for editors, referees, readers, and listeners alike, while communication should become more of a reality than it is today.

December 1984

Stephen Lock
Editor, British Medical Journal

Contents

Contributors

Denis M. Burley, MB, BS, FRCP
Head of International Medical Liaison, Ciba-Geigy Pharmaceuticals Division, Horsham, West Sussex, England

Clifford Hawkins, MD, FRCP
Honorary Consultant Physician to the Queen Elizabeth Hospital, Birmingham, and Senior Clinical Lecturer to the University of Birmingham, England

David A. Heath, FRCP
Reader in the Department of Medicine, University of Birmingham, England

Stanley R. Jenkins, BA
Assistant Librarian, The Barnes (Medical) Library, The Medical School, University of Birmingham, England

Martin J. Kendall, MD, FRCP
Senior Lecturer in Clinical Pharmacology, Department of Therapeutics and Clinical Pharmacology, Queen Elizabeth Hospital, Edgbaston, Birmingham, England

Jane Smith, BA
Staff Editor, British Medical Journal, London

Marco Sorgi, MD, MASVS
Consultant Surgeon of the Venezuelan Health Service, Senior Lecturer (Ad Honorem), School of Medicine, Caracas, Venezuela

William F. Whimster, MD, FRCP, FRCPath
Reader and Honorary Consultant in Morbid Anatomy, King's College School of Medicine and Dentistry, Denmark Hill, London

1. Research: Why Do It?

David A. Heath

> *The faculties developed by doing research are those most needed in diagnosis.*
>
> F. H. Adler (1966)

Many are the motives for doing research. Some are tempted by the excitement of discovery — the chance of adding something new, however small, to the expanding frontier of knowledge. This may be an inherent feature of the human intellect and may explain much of the progress along the laborious road of biological evolution. A few have this quality in excess and are self-propelled; nor are they deterred by drudgery and disappointment, however great these may be. Others are stimulated by more mundane though important objectives: the pursuit of prestige or the need for publications due to the publish or perish pressure when climbing the ladder to a successful career.

Whatever the reason for undertaking research, the benefits are undoubted:

● A critical or scientific attitude is developed. The progress of medicine has been bedevilled by an empirical attitude. This has often been disastrous for the patient who, in the past, was subjected to blood letting, purging and mutilating and unnecessary operations like colectomy when the hypothesis of toxic foci held sway. The modern doctor, throughout his medical life, will have constantly to be assessing new approaches to the treatment of patients, whether these involve drugs, operations or new investigations. A knowledge of scientific methods and frequently the proper use of statistics is essential to evaluate such procedures.

● The chance to study a subject in depth.

● Getting to know how to use a library.

● Learning to assess the medical literature critically.

● Development of special interests and skills.

● Understanding the attitude of others whether in routine or research laboratories.

● Obtaining a higher degree.

Discovery – By Forethought and Serendipidity

New knowledge arises in various ways. It may originate in some quite unexpected observation which occurs during an ongoing investigation in an academic department — providing this is fully exploited. Opportunities come more often to active bench workers and to those involved in new techniques or with new equipment, for example an electron microscope.

Serendipidity is the faculty of making happy discoveries by accident and is derived from the title of the fairy tale *The Three Princes of Serendip,* the heroes of which were always making such discoveries. The role of chance in research has been discussed by several authors and many examples of discoveries where chance played a part are given by Beveridge (1950) in *The Art of Scientific Investigation.* James Austin (1978) in *Chase, Chance and Creativity* analysed the varieties of chance that contribute to creative events:

Chance i. This is the type of blind luck which can provide an opportunity to anyone motivated to do research. An example is the unexpected arrival of a patient with a rare metabolic disorder.

Chance ii. Here something has been added: action. Austin quotes Kettering, the automotive engineer, who stated "keep on going and the chances are that you will stumble on something, perhaps when you are least expecting it. I have never heard of anyone stumbling on something sitting down".

Paul Ehrlich provides a good example of this. He fervently believed in the possibility of a chemical cure for syphilis, persisting when all reasonable hope had gone — and finally succeeded with Salvarsan, the 606th compound to be tested. More recent was the discovery, for the first time, of a virus causing malignant disease in humans: Epstein and Barr persisted in spite of many failures in searching for this in the tissues of Burkitt's lymphoma, eventually culturing the cells and seeing the virus under the electron microscope.

Chance iii. Chance presents only a faint clue; the potential opportunity exists, but it will be overlooked except by that *one person* uniquely equipped to grasp its significance. As Louis Pasteur immortalised it, "Chance favours only the prepared mind". For example, although Sir Alexander Fleming discovered penicillin by serendipity in 1929, it was not until 1939 that Florey and Chain working at Oxford revealed its practical importance.

Chance iv. Here there is "*one* quixotic rider cantering in on his own homemade hobby horse to intercept the problem at an odd angle". This type of discovery is usually due to a combination of persistence and lateral thinking.

Historical Aspects

Every research worker should have some knowledge of the history of original investigation. Space does not allow more than mention of the landmarks, and many articles have been written about the remarkable information explosion due to research in this century (Weatherall 1981). Initially most medical research was started by individuals who spent many years either experimenting or collecting clinical information. One of the first to demonstrate the value of experimentation in clinical medicine was William Harvey (Fig. 1.1), who discovered the circulation of the blood in the seventeenth century. As with many of the great medical pioneers, he was ridiculed at the time and it was many years before the fundamental discoveries that he made affected medical thinking and practice.

The tradition of clinical observation at the bedside was far more popular than experimentation and this has been the mainstay of medical knowledge until the present century. One of the early proponents of this approach was Thomas Sydenham (Fig. 1.2), who has been called the 'English Hippocrates'. He started medicine late and qualified at the age of 39 after being a captain in Oliver Cromwell's army. He is justly famous for his studies of malarial fevers, dysentery, scarlet fever, measles and the chorea which bears his name. His best known work is his treatise on gout, from which he suffered. His account of hysteria, which he claimed affected half of his non-fever patients — today called psychosomatic disease — is a masterpiece of sober description. His

Fig. 1.1. William Harvey.

Fig. 1.2. Thomas Sydenham.

treatment was relatively reasonable and he based it on supporting the *vis medicatrix naturae* (the healing power of nature), though he did not escape entirely the temptation to do extensive blood letting. He also deserves credit because, although he was a puritan, he did adopt the new wonder drug, quinine, the "Jesuit powder", imported from Peru in the 1630s; apart from curing malaria (the most frequent disease of the time) this allowed it to be separated from other fevers.

The eighteenth century brought with it some of the first major therapeutic discoveries: William Withering (Fig. 1.3) of Birmingham, who was a clinician, botanist and social reformer, introduced digitalis into orthodox medicine after learning of the use of the plant foxglove for dropsy from an old woman in 1779; this clinical trial greatly advanced the treatment of patients with heart failure. A cure was found for scurvy and Jenner began his great work on vaccination against smallpox; he was a country doctor and had heard of the immunity against smallpox enjoyed by milkmaids who had previously been infected by cowpox. With the encouragement of his teacher, John Hunter, he started a research project on this and published his article in 1798, in which he demonstrated that inoculation with cowpox would produce protection against smallpox in man without ill effects to the patient. This has been of incalculable benefit to mankind, and the World Health Organisation has now found it possible to announce the 'eradication' of smallpox. Careful scientific work was beginning genuinely to benefit man.

Fig. 1.3. William Withering.

Fig. 1.4. Claude Bernard.

Fig. 1.5. Robert Koch.

The experimental approach of the eighteenth century waned in England in the nineteenth century and failed to sustain the impetus of the previous century, with most major contributions being descriptive ones (Booth 1979). However, on the continent, medical research was gaining momentum, particularly as microscopy developed. Claude Bernard's (Fig. 1.4) research greatly advanced our knowledge of human physiology and Pasteur performed experiments which indicated the existence of microorganisms as the cause of fermentation. Robert Koch (Fig. 1.5), who unlike Pasteur was medically qualified, subsequently proved that an organism could cause a specific disease. He used solid media and developed new methods of fixing and staining bacteria. Unfortunately, a wave of uncritical research then started, so he issued his famous postulates as criteria for further valid research: (1) The organism should be found in each case of the disease. (2) It should not be found in other diseases. (3) It should be isolated. (4) It should be cultured. (5) It should, when inoculated, produce the same disease. (6) It should be recovered from the inoculated animal. However, as in original work today, the ideal cannot always be achieved.

Research in the Twentieth Century

The present century began with medicine being predominantly a descriptive art with few effective remedies. Much was to change over the next 80 years, a great deal of which can be traced back to the development at the beginning of the century of specific medical research institutes which encouraged and financed full-time medical research. In the United States of America the Rockefeller Institute was created in 1901. In England, Sir Thomas Lewis (Fig. 1.6), working for the Medical Research Council, encouraged the development of clinical research as a career. Flexner (1912) commented on the educational systems in various countries and noted that most research appeared to be carried out in places where the staff worked full-time in the hospital or institution. This important

Fig. 1.6. Sir Thomas Lewis.

observation was noted by the Haldane Commission (1910–1913) and must have greatly influenced its members, for they then recommended the creation of full-time professors to direct academic or research departments. The greatest impetus for the rapid growth of medical science was the commitment by governments of major sums of public money to scientific medical research. The best example of this was the progressive development of the National Institutes of Health in America, which initiated research into widely ranging areas of medicine and the basic sciences.

The Information Explosion

Fredrickson (1981) has outlined the enormous developments of the past 30 years, when an exponential increase in our knowledge of the basic sciences has been matched by major advances in the treatment of patients and has enabled medicine to develop truly into both a descriptive and a therapeutic speciality. The very nature of these developments has brought with it tremendous problems. The range of most medical research is now so great as to be beyond the comprehension of the single person. Its cost has increased dramatically, leading to considerable problems in funding. More recently the potential commercial implications of university-based research have raised interesting new problems concerning the relationship between research institutes and profit-making organisations.

Financial Problems

Today we find scientific research threatened by the decreased affluence of the industrial nations. Research which in many areas has become increasingly expensive is having to share the pruning that is going on in most walks of life. Traditional sources of funds are being reduced. The various types of research and how these should be funded need to be discussed. Each may require a different type of research worker and different forms of research may be more appropriate for different countries, depending on their affluence and disease patterns.

Types of Research

Weatherall (1981) distinguishes between basic research, applied research and development, and clinical trials and the monitoring of the fruits of research in everyday use.

Basic Research

Basic research has been fundamental to most of the major medical advances ever made. It differs from all other forms of research in being totally unpredictable, and often there is no initial connection between the research and its medical application. Indeed, the most important scientific discoveries have been made by investigators pursuing their own ideas (Fredrickson 1982). Medical application may follow, but it may take a long time before this happens. Harvey's discovery of the circulation of the blood had no discernible effect upon medical practice for almost 300 years (Bearn 1981). By its very nature, basic research requires a major commitment from researchers who must have a good training in research techniques and in fields outside medicine. Results are unlikely to be achieved rapidly, so that a long-term commitment by those involved as well as by funding bodies is essential.

Unfortunately, the number of medically qualified people involved in this work appears to be falling, as in other areas of medical research. Physician post-doctoral researchers have declined from 65% of the total National Institute of Health trainees and fellows in 1970 to 30% in 1980 (Fredrickson 1981), and a similar change is probably taking place in Britain (Peart 1981). This is partly due to the increased complexity of medical research, though perhaps more importantly to the uncertainties of a career in research compared with medical practice and its greater remunerations; added to this is the increasing rigidity of undergraduate and postgraduate medical education, which makes it far more difficult to divert a significant amount of time to organising research. The enormous financial cost and complexity of basic research will probably demand that it becomes more and more localised to fewer big institutions, especially universities. Until possible practical applications emerge, the work is less likely to be supported by industry or private sources.

Applied and Developmental Research

Applied and developmental medical research must include a major contingent of medically qualified people to link the scientific advances to patient care. For this to be readily achieved, there will need to be close links, ideally physical, between the centres developing the new process and the patients; the linkage between universities and clinical medical schools is a good example of such a union. Wherever possible the nucleus of the development team would be medically qualified but also scientifically trained people. There is, however, a much greater possibility for doctors to spend a fruitful shorter period in research before returning to clinical practice. Such a scheme should ensure that the worker joined an established work team and thus was able to be educated in research techniques while following a proven field of interest.

Clinical Trials and Monitoring of Research Consequences

Clinical trials and monitoring the fruits of research in everyday clinical practice represent a different type of research work. By the time new developments have reached the clinical level, commercial organisations have usually become involved. This has various ramifications: first, the commercial organisation has a major commitment to having its product used, often even before its value has been demonstrated unequivocally; secondly, such an organisation often funds researchers to try to prove the value of the product, though all too frequently it fails to justify the original hopes when good evidence is obtained.

Audit on Research

Not surprisingly, there has been little "research on research". Comroe and Dripps, however, studied the research that led to ten major clinical cardiovascular and pulmonary advances between the period of 1945 and 1975 (Ringler 1977). Having decided on the key articles for these, they noted that over 40% of the research had a goal unrelated to the later clinical advance. Over 60% of the research was of a basic nature and nearly 70% had been performed in colleges, universities and medical schools. In almost 60% of cases it took over 20 years for the original research to lead to the clinical advance. This study highlights the need to continue to support basic research which usually will not be specifically directed at clinical problems. The link of basic research to clinical institutes is also stressed as being essential for the appropriate application of advances to patient care. The information produced by this report also suggests that further "research on research" may be fruitful.

Who Should Do Research?

The question is whether all doctors or merely a selected few should perform research. Obviously not all doctors can be involved in basic research; this occupies virtually all of the person's time for a considerable duration and the fact that much of the work will be far removed from clinical practice may make it an unsuitable field for those wishing to spend a short time in full-time research. Furthermore, the need for the research worker to be appointed for prolonged periods in itself poses problems, for the most innovative and active phase of a research worker's life is likely to be during his or her younger years — "if you block the tide of the young coming in, you destroy the vitality of science" (Fredrickson 1982). To date we have not been able to devise a scheme for dealing with the research worker who is no longer as productive, though not yet ready to retire. As stated earlier, it is likely that more and more basic research will be carried out in fewer, larger institutes. Funding will be predominantly from governmental resources, with industry playing a minor role. These full-time investigators ideally will be left to pursue their own ideas with often no obvious benefits to patients in mind. Some medically qualified people will enter such areas but they will probably retain little if any contact with patients.

The vast majority of medically qualified doctors will want to spend a major part of their time in active clinical practice and only devote 2 or 3 years to part-time or full-time research, preferably in a laboratory.

Should All Doctors Do Some Research?

There is a strong argument that all doctors should do some research even if they wish to spend the rest of their lives dealing with patients. A scientific approach is essential, for, as medicine advances rapidly, so the need for a more critical evaluation of new developments becomes more urgent. The more potent the treatments or new procedures we develop, the greater the chances of benefit *and* harm to the patient. The medical past is littered with example after example of possible major advances eventually being shown to be of no value or, much worse, of positive harm to the patient. Despite these warnings, the medical profession and the general public seem to wish to try more and more unproven treatment. The problems of the past are likely to keep repeating themselves unless a far greater critical attitude develops within our profession. Hence for medical advances to continue, research will always need to be done, and for the high standards of medicine to be applied a carefully developed critical mind is needed. This is most likely to be developed in a research environment. Here the doctor will be constantly exposed to the critical evaluation of previous work, the design of good projects and the discipline of writing up observations. Also, the opportunity to review papers under supervision often arises; this greatly adds to the ability to evaluate new claims more carefully, as do the rigours of presenting work to a critical audience.

References

Adler FH (1966) Trans Am Acad Ophthalmol and Otolaryngol 70:17

Austin JH (1978) Chase, chance and creativity: The lucky art of novelty. Columbia University Press, New York

Bearn AG (1981) The pharmaceutical industry and academe: Partners in progress. Am J Med 71:81–88

Beveridge WB (1950) The art of scientific investigation. Heinemann, London

Booth CC (1979) The development of clinical science in Britain. Br Med J 1:1469–1473

Flexner A (1912) Medical education in Europe. A report to the Carnegie Foundation for the advancement of teaching. Bulletin No. 6

Fredrickson DS (1981) Biomedical research in the 1980s. N Engl J Med 304:509–517

Fredrickson DS (1982) 'Venice' is not sinking (the water is rising). Some views on biomedical research. JAMA 247:3072–3075

Peart WS (1981) Advice from a not so young medical scientist. Clin Sci 61:364–368

Report to the Royal Commission on University Education in London (1910–1913) Chairman, Haldane JS

Ringler RL (1977) The Comroe-Dripps report on the scientific basis for the support of biomedical science. Fed Proc 36:2564–2565

Weatherall M (1981) Medical research and national economics. J R Soc Med 74:407–408

2. Planning and Protocol

Martin J. Kendall and Clifford Hawkins

> *If an idea presents itself to us, we must not reject it simply because it does not agree with the logical deductions of a reigning theory.*
>
> Claude Bernard

Planning Research

Planning the research project is probably the most important aspect of all. This decides the whole future of the investigation. If the plan is good, all may go well. If the plan is not thought out carefully, the work may never be completed. Time employed in setting up a good plan is well spent and saves time which could be wasted in trying to patch up a bad one later. This is summed up well by Edward J. Huth (1982), editor of the *Annals of Internal Medicine,* "The probability that a paper with a clear image will emerge from research is determined more by how the research was conceived and planned than by how well the paper is written. A clear question must be posed before the research is planned, the design of the research plan must be adequate, and the data must be properly collected and appropriately analyzed".

Birth of an Original Idea

Research often starts from an idea, a question or an extension of a previous line of enquiry. The first thoughts are often vague and rather grandiose, tending to overestimate the resources available and underestimate the time needed to complete the project. However, without optimism much research would never be started. Adequate planning and preparation of a proper protocol are essential and the following questions must be considered:

1. Is the Idea Viable? Research should be "the art of the soluble" (Scott 1981). There is often a tendency to tackle problems of far too great a magnitude, such as an attempt to determine whether the rarity of rheumatic fever in the western world is due to antibiotics or social conditions. The idea should usually be simple and the objectives of the research circumscribed and definite.

2. Is It Practical?   An enthusiastic novice may easily waste time on contemplating a project that is impossible. For example, the idea may require work using an electron microscope or a difficult assay; unless you have an expert to join you, it may take months or even years to master a difficult laboratory technique. Or a retrospective study needing the perusal of 100 casenotes of patients may be conceived; but before starting, a survey of a sample of the casenotes must be done to make sure that the evidence is forthcoming, as so often they are haphazard and badly written. The animals or patients may not be available so you could wait a long time, for example, to find ten patients with Crohn's disease who have an ileostomy. Some ideas are good but would need scores of workers and several years to complete — or the cost would be too great for the budget.

3. The Time Factor.   Research needs time, so make sure that you will have time away from routine commitments to work in peace and carry it out. Also consider how long it is likely to take, for the average research grant lasts only 3 years.

4. Has It Been Done Before?   It is easy for the beginner to become disillusioned. He gets an idea, goes to the library, looks up the literature and finds that much has already been done on this subject. Hence the well-known scientist Medawar (1969) suggested to the young scientist that too much reading too early would stifle attempts at research. Even if the idea has already been investigated, it is worth thinking about this further as the method of previous workers may have been unreliable or it could be worthwhile to repeat it or to extend the idea.

5. What Result Is Expected?   This is worth considering though it is often unpredictable. Make sure that any result is liable to be worthwhile even if a negative result is obtained. Also, bear in mind whether it is likely to be accepted for publication by a medical journal.

6. What Do Colleagues Think?   It is worth discussing the idea with a colleague, especially one who is an expert in the field. Also, those who do research tend to imagine that they are working in isolation and are frequently surprised to discover that others either in the University or elsewhere are doing similar or related types of research. Contact with such people may be of great help in broadening the worker's knowledge of the literature, in obtaining advice about techniques and methods, and also in gaining access to a particular machine or a suitable method which may be of great assistance.

The appropriate expert may be working at some distant laboratory. Nevertheless it may be well worthwhile trying to contact the person, especially if the research requires setting up some new method of measuring something or performing a difficult procedure. Although one can read the instructions given in a published paper, this is never so helpful as discussing the practical problems either face to face or on the telephone. Sometimes it is best to go and watch the expert carrying out the technique.

However, do not be put off just by scepticism. "Neophobia" — fear of new ideas — is common; new ideas tend to be opposed and turned down.

7. Will a Statistician Be Needed?   The word statistics is liable to cause a mental block in some people, or a statistician is called in after the work has been completed to try and obtain significant values from the results. However, it is always preferable to have discussions with a statistician at the start so as to forecast how many measurements and how many patients may be needed and to consider variables that may influence the results. He or she may also have good ideas on how the results should be recorded to facilitate statistical analyses at the end. Experts may be at hand, especially if the work has been done in a university, and pharmaceutical firms usually have this specialised knowledge available for those carrying out drug trials. However, statistics must never be used to infer "cause and effect" relationships, even when there is a high correlation between the two.

8. What Will You Do?   Do indicate how much practical work you yourself are going to do. It is easy for a doctor to concoct an idea and sit aloof, letting others do all the work. Filling out forms for laboratory investigations hardly justifies the term personal research. Work at the bench is an invaluable discipline and an unexpected result may stimulate new ideas (Fig. 2.1).

Writing the Plan (Research Protocol)

Planning should be directed towards producing a written protocol. This is essential for several reasons: it forces the planner to define precisely his aim and objectives, the nature of the measurements to be made, the population or animal group to be studied and the way in which he hopes to interpret the results. In addition, it ensures that all involved on the

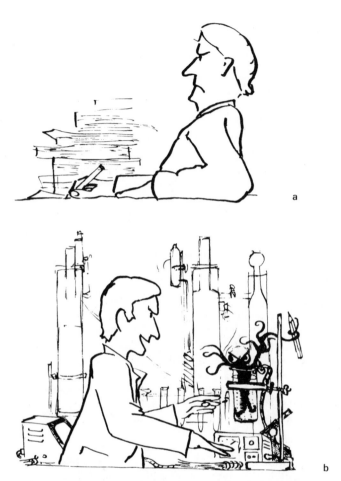

Fig. 2.1. a Filling out forms hardly justifies the term personal research. **b** Work at the bench is an invaluable discipline and an unexpected result may stimulate new ideas.

project have a clear idea of the aims to be achieved and procedures to be adopted.

The object must be to produce a sufficiently clear and detailed protocol which may be used by all those involved in the study, which could be submitted to an ethical committee and which forms the basis for applying for a research grant or even for the final report. The preparation of such a document frequently stimulates the researcher to make more detailed arrangements and to discuss the details with others. These moves may prove to be very important in the planning of the project.

15

Format of the Protocol

The protocol should be type-written, double-spaced on three or four pages of A4 paper — the shorter and more concise it is, the more likely it is to be read. Headings should be clearly laid out as follows:

Background.   One or two paragraphs should explain the background against which the work is to be performed and set out the results of any previous studies related to the research to be undertaken. Any person who reads the brief background should be left with a clear understanding of how the new study follows on from the current state of knowledge and why it needs to done. References (up to about ten) can be given at the end.

Aims of the Study.   The aim or object of the study should be set out succinctly.

The Basic Organisation.   This should include one or two sentences setting out (a) the investigators, giving the names of those specifically involved in the study whose names will appear in any publications, (b) the place where the study is to be performed and (c) the time when it is hoped to start the study and possibly its likely duration.

Materials.   The materials to be investigated or used should be clearly defined and details given of their quantity, quality and source if this is appropriate. This section may apply to patients when a drug trial (see later) is being performed.

Plan of the Investigation.   As far as is possible, details should be given concerning the start of the investigation and how long it is likely to continue. In this section the investigator should set out exactly what he or she intends to do. Depending upon the nature of the project it may be necessary to specify time, places, frequency of dosing or sampling. The nature and timing of all measurements should be stated.

End of Protocol.   References should be given accurately and in detail (see Chap. 5); these will refer to work quoted. Also, when the protocol has been typed, the date should be added and it may be useful to indicate that it is the first draft. Frequently, as a result of reviews by other members of a team and the ethical committee when patients are involved, modifications have to be made. This means that there may be three or more versions of the protocol. Confusion is likely to arise if some of the investigators are using the first version, some the second and some the third — so put the number or date on each.

Collecting and Recording Data

A rigid notebook discipline must be developed from the start. Every detail must be recorded neatly and legibly. A large book is often useful as it is less likely to be lost. Anyway, this is valuable and must be kept in a safe place, preferably locked up; indeed, some cautious souls will keep a duplicate set of records locked up elsewhere, and even less cautious workers should keep duplicate copies of key results. Photocopying facilities now make this very easy.

Further ideas concerning the work may come to mind at any time of night or day or arise during a conversation with a colleague, or someone may suggest a reference or someone to contact. A pocket notebook is useful for this purpose. Alternatively a pack of record cards can be kept in one pocket and when one is used for noting down something, it is transferred to another pocket — the pending pocket which can be emptied at the end of each day and the cards filed.

Recording Results for Analysis

A decision concerning how to classify and code results should be taken at the start. This is especially necessary when collecting data from patients. For example, a visual analogue scale may be used to assess the effect of an analgesic on pain; or a questionnaire may be sent to patients to collect information. The latter was used in a study of patients' reactions to their investigations (Hawkins 1979): a large number of questions were put to the patient by the interviewer and much time had to be spent on the coded questionnaire before using it; then a small pilot trial was done to assess its feasibility. Each question had to be subdivided, for example "Was the test explained to you?" was coded no - 0, yes - 1, partly - 2, previous knowledge - 3. Although 504 patients were studied, the amount of information was not considered large enough to need a computer, so it was analysed by hand using Hollerith cards and a sorter.

Coding

Coding merely means the allocation of a different symbol, usually a number, to each piece of information; as in the above example, verbal information is converted to numbers.

Method of Recording Data

When the number of individuals being studied is not very large and the information obtained not very great, data can be transferred onto cards. Suitable record cards are those with a series of holes in the margin; each hole is designed to represent one detail and this detail is recorded by punching the card and tearing the flap between the hole and the margin of the card. It is, of course, possible to make one's own simple card by using a postcard or record card, putting heavy pencil or pen markings at the card edge; these also stand out when a pack of records are stacked together for sorting. The proper edge-punched card is sorted out using a knitting needle.

The centre-punched card needs more elaborate machinery for both preparation and sorting. Its advantage is that it can carry more information than an edge-punched card; it has to be punched on one machine and sorted out on another which may also count whilst sorting. These cards have 80 columns of figures, each offering a choice of 12 positions for punching, and professional punch-card operators can prepare as many as 200 cards in an hour. The sorting machine takes nearly 10 minutes to sort 500 cards for one item of information, so analyses involving anything other than simple breakdowns and correlations become rather time consuming. Punch-cards prepared for a Hollerith sorter can also provide the raw material for transfer to magnetic tape for computer analysis, and information on magnetic tape can be returned to punch-cards for storage.

The computer is invaluable for storing and analysing large amounts of data and does so within a few seconds. Its drawbacks lie in the risk of the machine breaking down and the need to wait for access to it or to make way for "emergencies"; it also can be expensive, and writing and checking a program can be difficult and time consuming.

The Pilot Run

Doing a trial study beforehand is often worthwhile; for example, if a new drug is to be tested, a study of a few patients may indicate whether it is worthwhile or not, before complicated protocols are developed. In any research, problems may be discovered at this stage and solved before the work is started and time wasted.

Is the Research Ethical?

This question must be considered whenever patients or volunteers are needed for research. In many countries, the plan has to be submitted to a Research Ethical Committee which may consist of a chairman (usually medical), two or three doctors, an administrator, a member of the nursing staff and a lay person. The purpose of this is to protect the patient from unethical procedures because they are either too unpleasant or dangerous and to protect the doctor in case any legal problems should arise. Some ethical committees also consider the quality of the research, for bad research is itself immoral and unethical as it usually puts the patient to unnecessary discomfort or pain, and causes waste of his time and even loss of time from work.

Applying for a Research Grant

Writing an application to obtain money for a project needs great care. Indeed the application for funds has been described as "grantmanship: an exercise in lucid presentation" (Merritt 1963), and when grants are not approved this is often due to faults in the application (Allen 1960). It must be written clearly and concisely and preferably be typed. Fortunately most bodies providing research funds issue a suitable form and this should be applied for.

The usual format is:

Title page. This should provide a short descriptive title, the applicant's name and address, and the date of submission.

The introduction states a short summary of the research problem with a few references to previous work. Questions can be posed which you hope to answer. These can be provocative as this can be more likely to stimulate interest.

Materials (or patients) and methods. Details should be given, for example, of the number and type of patients and methods to be used; if a method is in routine use, then no more than a reference to a paper describing it is needed, but exact and precise details of a new method must be given.

Facilities available. This section concerns the availability of laboratory space and special techniques, and the possibility of liaison with other departments such as in a university. The names of colleagues who have been consulted and will provide special knowledge or technical help should also be mentioned. It is particularly important, if a difficult technique is being developed, to have access to a well-known expert.

The site where the research will be done must be stated. This may be at a bench in a certain laboratory, the permission of the director having been obtained.

Finances needed should be clearly set out in detail, usually on a yearly basis. The cost of materials, travelling expenses for patients and so on, animals and their husbandry and anything else must be written out. The finance needed can be divided into (1) capital costs and (2) current (running) expenses.

References must be typed out accurately as it is very irritating when the donor of a grant cannot look them up properly. There need be only six to ten but they must be relevant and preferably, though not necessarily, recent.

Finally, the curriculum vitae of the applicant must be included and also be neatly set out. A successful applicant will have written clearly and concisely the answer to four questions (Calnan 1976):

Why do I want to do this? ...   the need
What do I want to do? ....   the plan
How am I going to do it? ....   the method
What do I need? ....   the resources

The application should be re-read to check these points before sending it off. Applications to grant-giving bodies are assessed by a committee and sometimes sent to experts for their assessment. The following five questions will be considered when the application is studied:

1. Is the idea important?
2. Can it be done?
3. Is the applicant competent to do the work?
4. Can it be done within the specified time?
5. Are the costs realistic?

Reasons for an Application Being Rejected

Applications may be turned down because the scientific merit of the idea is not worthwhile, because the applicant has not taken sufficient trouble to plan or think about the project, because too much reliance is being placed on others to do most of the work — or, of course, because too much money is being asked for.

Planning a Clinical Trial

Clinical trials must be planned as for other research. A planning team should think out what they want to do and produce a protocol. When assessing the effects of drugs, the team would normally include somebody from the pharmaceutical industry — preferably a scientific member of the medical department; then information about the drug, expertise on clinical trial methodology, suitably packaged drugs, booklets for data recording and access to a statistician may all be provided. Most would not consider doing a clinical trial without such support. On the other hand a more marketing-orientated person may well try to persuade you to perform a study which purports to be a trial but is little more than a drug-promoting exercise and an enticement to persuade you to use the drug.

Having decided to do a trial, and having formulated a precise question to be answered and the patient group to be studied, the next step is to decide what sort of trial is required.

Open, Uncontrolled Trials

Open, uncontrolled trials are used to decide whether the drug appears to be effective and to determine what dose is required to produce the desired effect. They will also indicate how well or badly the drug is tolerated. The term *open* means that both patients and doctors know what is being taken and the term *uncontrolled* means that the potentially active substance is not being compared with anything. In this way a new drug X may be given to patients with angina at a dose of say 10, 20, 30 and then 40 mg daily to see whether X appears to reduce the frequency or severity of the attacks of chest pain. In this context a reduction of the angina could be a placebo effect or it could mean that the drug made the patients too ill to want to move very much. In other words, this type of trial is a poor guide to efficacy but is a necessary preliminary step before proceeding to more demanding controlled trials. Certainly lack of improvement suggests that either the drug is ineffective or the dose inadequate.

The open, uncontrolled trial, whether consisting of a large number of patients or merely a few (the pilot trial), must never be accepted as putting the stamp of certainty on the value of any drug. These trials have notoriously been misleading and have resulted in the futile and dangerous use of drugs on a large scale — often promoted irresponsibly by the pharmaceutical industry, which naturally wishes to sell the new drug and does not have evidence from controlled trials.

Controlled Trials

Controlled trials are designed to determine efficacy by comparing the new drug with a placebo or at a later stage with the standard comparator substance such as indomethacin or aspirin for anti-inflammatory analgesics or propranolol for β-blockers. *Single blind* implies that the patient is unaware what tablets are being taken but the doctor knows. This may be necessary if the dose has to be titrated to achieve the desired result or if some specific side-effect has to be looked for. However, in single-blind trials there is a real possibility that some kind of bias may influence the doctor's assessment. It may not affect the haemoglobin or the blood sugar but it may well influence the way the blood pressure is reported or adverse reactions are recorded. If careful monitoring is required it is preferable that the person who regulates the tablets does not make the recordings related to tolerability or efficacy. *Double-blind trials* (when the doctor is ignorant as well) using tablets prepacked by some third party undoubtedly offer the best chance of obtaining a meaningful unbiased comparison.

Trial Design

Most trials use either a *comparative group* or a *cross-over design*. Comparative groups involve treatment X to group A and treatment Y to group B. This sort of comparison must be used if we are treating an acute condition. One disadvantage is that it is wasteful of patients, volunteers or animals because only half can have each treatment. More important, it assumes that the two groups are comparable in aspects related to prognosis and responsiveness (relevant factors). It is obviously important that when assessing a new form of steroid enema for ulcerative colitis, the two groups should be comparable in terms of extent of disease, since distal colitis has a much better prognosis. When following patients after a myocardial infarction there are so many relevant factors (age, sex, smoking habit, heart failure etc.) that one requires huge numbers to obtain a reasonable balance. In some conditions such as rheumatoid arthritis, the variation of the disease in different patients is greater than that expected from the non-steroidal anti-inflammatory drugs used in treating it (Scott et al. 1982). Generally, the smaller the effect expected from a drug when compared with a placebo or another drug, the larger the number of patients needed for the trial.

In cross-over trials group A starts with treatment X and then changes to treatment Y, whilst group B has the treatments in the reverse order. In this type of trial all the patients have both treatments and they all act as their own control. Cross-over trials are ideally suited for chronic conditions, for example rheumatoid arthritis, Parkinson's disease or disseminated sclerosis. The problems here are (1) that there may be an order effect, (2) the first treatment may dramatically improve the condition or (3) the effects of the first treatment may persist and therefore overlap with the effects of the second treatment. The first two may be noted when the data are analysed. The third problem has to be anticipated and prevented by allowing an appropriate gap between the two courses of treatment.

Place, Time and Placebos

Meaningful information on a new drug or form of management will only be obtained if any effects observed can be ascribed to that alone. Since a patient may improve because someone takes an interest, or because they are admitted to hospital or the weather changes, care must be taken to ensure that comparisons are made between comparable groups under the same circumstances, at the same time. Comparisons between different institutions, the patients of different doctors and all retrospective studies, are suspect (but not necessarily meaningless).

Placebo tablets which can have marked therapeutic effects (Table 2.1) must match the active preparation in size, shape, colour and taste. If this is difficult then a double dummy technique is used. For example, if one set of tablets is white and the other blue then it may be necessary to have both white and blue placebos so that each dose consists of say two white and two blue tablets. Active tablets may also be recognised by both patients and doctors because of their actions or side-effects. Tricyclic antidepressants tend to cause dry mouth, blurred vision and drowsiness, whereas β-blockers cause bradycardia.

Is it ethical to use a placebo? It is clearly unethical to give a placebo alone to patients with a serious condition for which there is effective treatment, for example pneumococcal pneumonia. In other situations in which the disease is serious, such as myeloma, rheumatoid arthritis or disseminated sclerosis, we have to ask how effective is the best available treatment. If there is a fairly effective treatment it must be given and the

Table 2.1 Therapeutic effect of placebos (Jospe 1978)

Condition	Satisfactory relief
Rheumatic pains	34.9%
Migraine	32.3%
Sea sickness	58.0%
Cough relief	41.0%

new drug may be added to one group but not to the other. For disseminated sclerosis there is no effective therapy and therefore any new treatment should be tried against a placebo. Thus for less serious disorders and when effective therapy is not available, any new treatment has to start by being shown to be more effective and less harmful than doing nothing — which means giving a placebo.

Criteria for Inclusion and Exclusion

In any trial, the investigators must define the population they wish to study. This requires particular care if a multicentre trial is being performed. Do you want information on patients with indigestion or endoscopically biopsy proven gastric ulcer? Who should be excluded? In particular, what about age, renal function, pregnancy and other drugs?

Methods of Assessment

The statement that when a new anti-inflammatory drug was given to 58 patients with rheumatoid arthritis in ten centres, 77% had less pain and 82% less stiffness sounds good but is meaningless. How were pain and stiffness measured and were the techniques comparable at all ten centres? Rises in haemoglobin, falls in ESR and alterations in weight or left ventricular end-diastolic pressure may be more reliable markers of change. Falls in mortality are even more convincing.

In attempting to evaluate any new form of treatment, particularly for a relapsing and remitting disorder, we should look for objective measures of progress. We should also try to produce numerical data. A new hypnotic is more likely to be accepted if we can demonstrate that the mean duration of sleep was increased from 6.3 to 8.6 hours, a statistically significant increase. The alternative comment, that 58% said they had slept better on treatment A, is much less convincing, though it could be made to look convincing using a bold histogram.

Compliance

Failure to respond is frequently due to failure to take the tablets. It is obviously important in assessing a treatment to avoid failing to show benefit because of non-compliance. Checks can be made by adding perhaps seven more tablets than the patient needs and asking that the patient brings back the bottle when coming for the next one. Some drugs have measurable clinical or biochemical effects, for example they increase or lower heart rate, or they lower potassium. However, none of these is very satisfactory or widely applicable. Urine or blood sample analyses are reliable for the day of the visit but may be difficult, time consuming and expensive. The most effective approach to this problem is for the investigator to anticipate non-compliance and to instruct his patient carefully and frequently with this in mind.

Listing Adverse Effects

Almost all drugs may produce adverse effects and one aim of a trial is to assess their frequency and severity. In doing this it is important to remember two things. Firstly many patients (perhaps 20%) have minor symptoms (headache, lethargy, rashes, difficulty in sleeping etc.) when on *no* treatment. To be fair to the drug it is therefore necessary to assess these symptoms before treatment starts and/or whilst the patient is on a placebo. Secondly the incidence of side-effects will depend on how they are elicited. The number will usually be low if the doctor records only important side-effects which are volunteered spontaneously by the patient. They will be much higher if the patient quietly and privately fills in a long questionnaire. This latter will usually produce a long list of irrelevant minor symptoms but may be vital if one is looking for embarrassing effects like hirsutism in females or impotence in men. For multicentre trials it is obvious that the technique for eliciting and recording-side effects must be carefully standardised. The simple question "Have the tablets upset you in any way?" is a simple and acceptable way of finding out those side-effects which concern the patients.

Problems in Doing Drug Trials Properly

Research has been classified (see Chap. 1) as basic, applied and developmental, and clinical trials. Clinical trials have been discussed in this chapter as an example of problems involved in a research project because whereas the person involved in basic research will usually be a member of a team in an academic institution where criticism is easily available, clinical trials are often embarked upon without any previous research training. Also more clinical trials are now being undertaken than at any previous time. The rapid growth in new pharmaceutical products and medical research in other fields increases this demand. Unfortunately, drug trials are commonly done wrongly (Table 2.2) so that results are fallacious; this wastes doctors' time and inconveniences patients.

Table 2.2 Common errors in clinical trials

Too few patients (Altman 1980)
No controls — or unsatisfactory controls (Lionel and Herxheimer 1970)
Defaultors or drop-outs not included in the results
Bias
Faulty assessment
Wrongful use of a statistical method

Sir Austin Bradford Hill, the distinguished statistician, wrote: "Poorly constructed trials not only teach us nothing but may be dangerously misleading — particularly when their useless data are spuriously supported by all the latest statistical techniques and jargon. 'Blinding with science' becomes almost a meiosis.'' (Bradford Hill 1966).

An Example of a Futile Drug Trial

Assessing a New Anti-inflammatory Analgesic

You are invited to a film show extolling the virtues of a new drug for mild joint pain in rheumatic conditions. The method of action of the drug is explained in the film.

You are given a paper during the meeting which shows that in a trial of the drug in general practice 208 doctors were asked to give the drug to 1100 patients and to rate, after 4 weeks, the effects it had on their mobility and pain. The results were as follows:

		Less	The same	More	N
Mobility	— Female	38	67	577	700
	Male	26	41	212	400
Pain	— Female	553	79	44	700
	Male	228	31	20	400

This drug seems brilliantly effective but . . .! What questions would you want to ask about: (1) the patients, (2) the doctors, (3) the methods and (4) the trial plan — and other aspects? (Answers given opposite.)

1. **The patients.** There is no description of their age or of the exact diagnosis of the "rheumatic condition" or of how they were selected. The numbers do not add to 1100, so what happened to the drop-outs?

2. **The doctors.** The bias and observer's error amongst so large a number of doctors would render a trial useless. Who recruited the doctors? Was there any kind of reward for achieving a positive result?

3. **The method.** No mention is made of how mobility was measured, of how the degree of pain was assessed (such as by visual analogue scale) or of any side-effects. Were the techniques for making and recording all measurements standardised at each centre?

4. **The trial plan.** This is not mentioned. The absence of any controls means that the trial was futile. Inclusion of a statistician would, at least, have meant that the numbers in the table added up correctly.

A Warning for the Investigator

Before embarking on a clinical trial it is worth remembering that the law of general perversity (Murphy's law) applies, so:

● Even the simplist sounding trial can be difficult to carry out.

● Once the patient population to be studied has been defined, all such patients may disappear.

● The central figure in any clinical trial tends to leave or be ill when the trial is about to start.

● If it is essential that patients attend at certain precise times, they will appear at other times.

James Austin (1978) describes Murphy's law and some extrapolations as follows:

● If anything *can* go wrong it will.

● Left to themselves things always go from bad to worse.

● If there is a possibility of several things going wrong, the one that will go wrong is the one that will do you the most damage.

● Nature always sides with the hidden flaw.

● If anything seems to be going well, you have obviously overlooked something.

● Patrick's Theorem: If the experiment works, you must be using the wrong equipment.

● Homer's Five Thumb Postulate: Experience varies directly with the equipment ruined.

- Flagel's Law of the Perversity of Inanimate Objects: Any inanimate object, regardless of composition or configuration, may be expected to perform at any time in a totally unexpected manner for reasons that are entirely obscure or completely impossible.

- Allen's Axiom: When all else fails, read the instructions.

- Spare Parts Principle: The accessibility of small parts that fall from the work bench varies directly with the size of the part and inversely with its importance to the completion of your work.

- The Compensation Corollary: The experiment may be considered a success if no more than 50% of your observed results must be discarded to obtain a correlation with your hypothesis.

- Gumperson's Law: The probability of a given event happening is inversely proportional to its desirability.

- The Harvard Law: The experimental animal, brought up under strict genetic and environmental conditions, still reacts as it damn well pleases.

References

Allen EM (1960) Why are research grants disapproved? Science 132:1532–1534

Altman DG (1980) Statistics and ethics in medical research III. How large a sample? Br Med J 281:1336–1338

Austin J (1978) Chase, chance and creativity: The lucky art of novelty. Columbia University Press, New York

Bradford Hill A (1966) Reflections on the controlled trial. Ann Rheum Dis 25:107–113

Calnan J (1976) One way to do research: The A–Z for those who must. Heinemann, London

Hawkins CF (1979) Patients' reactions to their investigations: a study of 504 patients. Br Med J 3:638–640

Huth EJ (1982) How to write and publish papers in the medical sciences. ISI Press, Philadelphia

Jospe M (1978) The placebo effect in healing. Lexington Books, Toronto

Lionel NDW, Herxheimer A (1970) Assessing reports of therapeutic trials. Br Med J 2:637–640

Medawar PB (1969) Induction and intuition in scientific thought. Methuen, London

Merritt DH (1963) Grantmanship: an exercise in lucid presentation. Clin Res 11:375–377

Scott DF (1981) Research methods, especially in psychiatry. Br J Hosp Med December:596–602

Scott DL, Roden S, Marshall T, Kendall MJ (1982) Variations in responses to non-steroidal anti-inflammatory drugs. Br J Clin Pharmacol 14:691–694

3. Searching the Literature

S. R. Jenkins

> *Knowledge is of two kinds. We know a subject ourselves, or we know where we can find the information about it.*
>
> Dr. Samuel Johnson

The purposes of this chapter are to give the new research worker advice on the best way to acquire information and how to record it once found, and to describe the main sources of information available. At the start of your project, you will be spending a lot of time in the library. You should therefore, as early as possible, get to know your way about the library, become familiar with its layout, and, above all, make the acquaintance of the librarian. For the librarian is there to help you and is trained to know all about information sources and how to exploit them to the full. Guidance will be given on how to use the catalogue or to ferret out an obscure report which may be vital to the progress of your project.

The biomedical literature has grown to enormous proportions in the last few decades. Index Medicus, the main indexing journal in medicine, indexes almost 250 000 journal articles each year. In addition, the National Library of Medicine adds around 14 000 monographs and 2000 audiovisual items to its collection annually. Biological Abstracts, the largest abstracting journal in the life sciences, every year produces around 150 000 abstracts taken from over 9000 journals, any one of which may need to be consulted as likely to contain a paper of interest. To these must be added many thousands of theses, conference proceedings, research reports, statistical publications and newspapers which will contribute to the vast accumulation of literature often referred to as the information explosion (Fig. 3.1).

Fortunately the scientific literature, and particularly that of medicine and the life sciences, is well organised, and many indexes, catalogues and bibliographies exist to serve as access points to this vast store of knowledge. The remainder of this chapter will give you some guidance on the main sources of information; greatest emphasis will be given to journals (which you are most likely to use) and the principal abstracting and indexing services. A briefer account will be given of some other sources. Remember that each publication is unique and one often has advantages

Fig. 3.1. The information explosion — to these must be added many thousands of conference proceedings.

which the others do not. They all carry instructions on the most efficient method of using them and you should always study these carefully before embarking on your search.

Journals

Journals are regarded as the principal vehicle for the communication of scientific information and have two main advantages over other forms of literature. First, because of their frequency of publication they are able to provide *more recent information* than can be found in books, an important factor in such rapidly developing areas as immunology and pharmacology. Secondly, because they are the main channel of communication among scientists, they carry the latest and often very specific accounts of current research work, new techniques and unusual but interesting cases. The number of biomedical journals currently published is not easy to assess. A useful figure can be taken from the number being received by the National Library of Medicine, the most comprehensive library of its type in the world, which is around 22 000 (Fig. 3.2). Even when the many ephemeral items like house magazines and newsletters are subtracted from this total, there still remain a significant number of journals of importance.

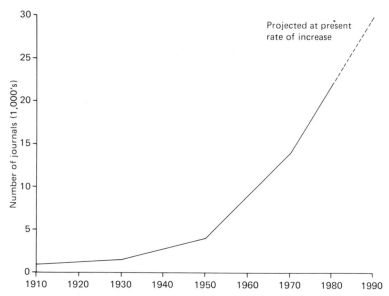

Fig. 3.2. Growth in the number of journals received at the National Library of Medicine.

Indexes and Abstracts

It is clearly impossible to assess the contents of journals by looking at each one individually (except for a limited period in a specialised subject), and so you need to make use of indexing and abstracting journals. An indexing journal is one which simply, by means of author and subject indexes, lists in a convenient way the contents of a number of other journals. An abstracting journal performs the same function but in addition provides an abstract or brief summary of the papers indexed, giving extra information and thereby enabling the user to establish at that point the possible value of the references found. Indexes and abstracts vary greatly in size, ranging from those like Index Medicus and Biological Abstracts which aim to cover the most significant journals in a wide subject, to those like Muscular Dystrophy Abstracts and Smoking and Health Bulletin which cover a much narrower field.

To search the literature by means of indexes and abstracts you should first select the one most relevant to your research interest; in doing this you would be well advised to act on the recommendation of your librarian or research supervisor. You should then, beginning with the most recent issue available, search under the subject headings of interest (see later) and continue backwards as far as you wish to go, making a note of any articles which seem to be of interest. Among the many articles found, you are likely to come across a number of review papers. These are especially valuable as they provide a good introduction to a subject and invariably have appended to them a list of further relevant references. Review papers are extremely important and, together with relevant monographs, form the first source to be read for you to acquire your basic information.

Your approach to the literature, then, should be methodical. You might begin with an article read in a current journal or with review papers or monographs and then proceed to articles giving more specific information. When this has been done, you will be equipped with enough background information to enable you to understand your own planned project and to put it into perspective before you begin your own work. This preparatory search of the literature is of extreme importance and should not be passed over lightly. Time spent in the library is time well spent.

Recording Information by Keeping Adequate Records

Make sure that you record every relevant piece of information. It is a common and frustrating problem to find that after an article has been written, a reference which has been read and is invaluable, is missing. Then much time is wasted, perhaps by looking through scribbled notes or by starting again in the library to find it. The best method of avoiding this is to use record cards, those measuring 10×15 cm being the most suitable. On each card you should record sufficient information to enable you to locate the reference when you next need it and this will also serve when you eventually produce a bibliography of references at the end of your own publication.

The details needed for books consist of author (or editor), title, edition (if any), place of publication, publisher and publication date, e.g.

> Walton, J.N. (ed.)
> Disorders of voluntary muscle. 2nd ed.
> London, Churchill, 1969

For a journal article the information required is author(s), title of paper, name of journal (*in full*), date, volume and inclusive page numbers, e.g.

> Brown, D.D.
> Gene expression in eukaryotes.
> Science, 1981, *221*, 666–674

Fig. 3.3. Record cards for recording references.

A reference to a chapter in a book should be a combination of these and should be presented in this way:

> Roberts, D.C.
> The organisation of personal index files.
> In: Morton, L.T. (ed.) Use of medical literature. 2nd ed.
> London, Butterworths, 1977, pp. 441–452

In addition to this information you can also use these record cards to contain comments as to whether the reference is good, average or non-informative. They easily fit into a pocket and can be carried around so that they are always available. Later they can be filed into a box (Fig. 3.3), a keyword perhaps being written on the top line to facilitate filing.

In addition to gathering and indexing references to which you are likely to refer in the future, it can also be valuable to build up a collection of reprints and photocopies of interesting articles, particularly if you feel you will refer to them frequently or if they are in journals not easily accessible to you. Again, many methods of storing these are possible. Most papers can be easily stored in boxes but they should be filed in such a way that they can be quickly located when needed. Filing by subject is one possibility but this permits filing under one heading only. Other methods include filing under author's name or under journal title.

The simplest way is to link the storage of these papers with your file of references since, as the paper must be of interest to you for you to have bothered to acquire a copy, you have also recorded the reference in your file. As each new reprint is added to your collection you place them in boxes and number them sequentially. Your index card can be clearly marked with the number of the reprint and when at a later date you find the reference to this in your file you will be quickly alerted to the fact that you have a copy of that particular reference in your own collection.

A good rule is always to include *the inclusive* pages of the paper. If they are not needed later, you can always omit them; but if you have not recorded them at the start, it can be very time consuming to try to locate these details at a later date when you are itching to send off the article. Unnecessary bother can be avoided by writing down your references accurately as you go along.

Sources of Information and How to Use Them

A lot of your time is going to be spent in the library; you should therefore try to find out as much about it as you can. After all, it will play as important a role as the laboratory in the early stages of your work. Get to know what services are offered and see how many will be beneficial to you; try to understand the way the stock is arranged, particularly the location of the sources you will be using most frequently; and, most important, find out how to use the catalogues which are the vital key to the library's holdings. Remember that if your approach to the library is not methodical you are unlikely to obtain everything you need.

Journals

Journals will be arranged according to subject or, more simply, alphabetically by title. A catalogue of journal holdings is usually available on cards or in book form and this should be consulted to establish that the title you are looking for is held in your library. This journal holdings list will consist of an alphabetical list of titles held, together with details of the particular volumes carried.

A brief description of how these holdings are expressed could be useful:

New England Journal of Medicine 198– 1928–

This shows that the first volume of New England Journal of Medicine held in the library is volume 198, published in 1928. The dash and the space following it indicate that the library still subscribes to this journal and holds all volumes since the initial date.

Humangenetik   1–30   1964–1975
Continued by: Human Genetics

From this we learn that the journal Humangenetik is held in the library from volume 1, published in 1964, to volume 30, published in 1975. We are also advised here of a change of title; that is, that after volume 30 the title became Human Genetics, and if we look this title up in the holdings list we find

Human Genetics   31–   1976–

which again shows us that this title is being received currently.

Where the library has incomplete holdings of a particular title you will come across an entry like this:

Journal of Physiology   1–22   1878–1896;   44–87
                      1911–1932;   109–   1946–

from which we know that the Journal of Physiology is held only between volumes 1 and 22, and between 44 and 87, but continuously since volume 109. Once you are used to it the journal holdings list is easy to use. When you have checked and confirmed that the title you need is held in your library it is then an easy matter to find the correct volume on the shelf and the page on which your required paper appears.

Books

To trace a book you should first look in the library catalogue. Mention of the catalogue often tends to cause alarm in the average user who prefers to avoid it and restrict his use of the library to those books which he can find by looking around the shelves. It cannot be stressed too strongly that you should get to know how to use the catalogue because it is the only complete record of the library's stock and the library cannot be used efficiently without it.

Library catalogues come in many shapes and sizes; they may be on cards or in sheafs, and nowadays they are frequently found in microform so that it is very difficult to generalise about them. Whatever their format, however, they do enable you to find books according to authors, subjects and occasionally titles.

A type of catalogue that is often encountered is known as a dictionary catalogue, where entries for both names and subjects are listed in a single alphabetical sequence, e.g.

Brasher, P.L.
Breast
Bright's Disease
British Medical Association
Brown, K.L. *ed.*
Brucellosis

In some catalogues the entries for names and subjects are filed in separate sequences. Note, incidentally, that names include not only authors, but also editors, compilers and translators, names of societies and organisations, and even names of conferences and symposia.

When you have found the catalogue entry for the book you are looking for you will see that, in addition to giving you the full publication details, it will also carry a shelfmark in a prominent position. This shelfmark is a link between the catalogue and the shelves and indicates the location of the books within the library.

You may on occasion come across what is known as a classified catalogue, which replaces the alphabetically arranged subject catalogue. Here the entries are filed according to the classification used in the library and to use this type of catalogue properly you first need to know the classmark of the subject you are looking for.

A classification scheme widely used throughout the world is the Dewey Decimal Classification, which employs a numerical notation and divides the whole field of knowledge into ten main classes numbered from 000 to 999. In this scheme the numbers 610 to 619 are allocated to medicine and all medical books will therefore be found within this range. Individual classmarks for specific subjects are built up from these classmarks by the addition of extra numbers, as this example shows:

610	Medicine
611	Anatomy
616	Internal medicine
616.4	Endocrinology
616.462	Diabetes

Use of a classification scheme like this (and most schemes work in the same way although the notation may be different) means first that all books on the same subject have the same classmark; in this case all books on diabetes would carry the classmark 616.462. It also means that books on related subjects are shelved near to each other; all books on aspects of endocrinology, for example, would bear a classmark beginning 616.4. To establish the classmark of your subject is then an easy matter. Near the catalogue you will find a subject index which is an alphabetical list of terms followed by their classmarks. By looking up

"Diabetes" in the subject index you will see that its classmark is 616.462 and if you then look under this classmark in the catalogue you will find a complete list of the library's books on the subject.

If your library is of moderate size it will probably be able to provide you with most books and journals you need from its own stock. No library, however, is comprehensive and even the largest is unlikely to contain all the items you require. If your library does not hold an item you want, you should make use of the interlibrary loan service. Most countries now have a network whereby libraries requiring a book not in their own stock are able to borrow it from another. The service is usually efficient and means that much of your reading can be made available from other libraries in your own country or even from libraries abroad. Often these interlibrary loans will be supplied as photocopies since they are much cheaper to post; occasionally they come in microform, but this should present no problem since most libraries own suitable equipment to read them.

Index Medicus

Index Medicus is produced by the National Library of Medicine and indexes the contents of around 2700 of the world's most important medical journals. Each monthly issue consists of articles indexed by both subject and author; at the end of the year these issues are combined to form the Cumulated Index Medicus.

Figure 3.4 shows part of the subject section of Index Medicus and lists articles that have appeared on toxic hepatitis. Note first that a full bibliographical reference is provided. The title of the journal is given in an abbreviated form. In most cases you will find it easy to work out from this the full journal title; in cases of difficulty you can consult the List of Journals Indexed, which is included in the January issue of the Index Medicus. This consists of a list of the abbreviations followed by the full title of the journal.

Returning to Fig. 3.4, you will see that many titles of the papers are enclosed in square brackets. This shows that although the title is given here in English, the article is in another language, which is indicated by a three letter code at the end of the reference. Many foreign language papers contain an abstract in English; if so it is shown by the note "Eng. Abstr.", which precedes the language abbreviation. One other point to note is the use of subheadings such as etiology, metabolism, occurrence etc. There are over 60 of these and they primarily serve to break up what could otherwise be an unwieldy list of references and to help you to locate quickly specific aspects of the main subjects and thereby avoid looking through a long list of irrelevant references.

HEPATITIS, TOXIC

Multiple attacks of jaundice associated with repeated sulfonamide treatment. Iwarson S, et al. **Acta Med Scand** 1979;206(3):219-22

DIAGNOSIS

[Skin hypersensitivity test] Chujo T. **Nippon Rinsho** 1979 Jun 29;Suppl:2416-7 **(Jpn)**
[Challenge test] Furusawa S. et al. **Nippon Rinsho** 1979 Jun 29;Suppl:2418-9 **(Jpn)**
[Blastoid transformation reaction and MI test (LMI test)] Mizoguchi Y. **Nippon Rinsho** 1979 Jun 29;Suppl:2420-3 **(Jpn)**

DRUG THERAPY

Effects of cicloxilic acid on CCl4-induced liver injury. Bramanti G, et al. **Arzneim Forsch** 1978;28(7a):1212-7

ENZYMOLOGY

Serum enzymes as indicators of chemically induced liver damage. Drotman RB, et al. **Drug Chem Toxicol** 1978; 1(2):163-71

ETIOLOGY

Reductive metabolism of halothane and hepatotoxicity [letter] Cousins MJ. **Anesthesiology** 1979 Nov;51(5):486
Cocaine-induced hepatic necrosis in mice--the role of cocaine metabolism. Thompson ML. et al. **Biochem Pharmacol** 1979 Aug 1;28(15):2389-95
Histopathological alterations induced by uranyl nitrate in the liver of albino rat. Goel KA, et al.

Fig. 3.4. Part of subject section of Index Medicus.

Index Medicus is a well-produced index and convenient to use. However, you should be warned never to attempt to search it without first establishing the correct heading or headings under which papers are indexed. There are around 16 000 of these and they are published every year in a volume called Medical Subject Headings which appears in the second part of the January issue of Index Medicus. These headings, generally known as MeSH headings, form the authoritative list of terms under which articles appear in Index Medicus and an understanding of their use is essential for the efficient use of Index Medicus.

MeSH is divided into two sections — the alphabetic list and the tree structures. Figure 3.5 shows part of the alphabetic list in which all MeSH headings, together with cross-references, are listed in alphabetical order.

The first point to notice from this list is that the only headings which will be used as MeSH headings under which papers will appear in Index Medicus are those printed in large capitals., e.g. GIGANTISM and GINGIVA. The remaining headings, in smaller type, are cross-references and these are of two sorts. The first consists of a straightforward

GIBBERELLINS
D11.303.760.408

GIBBON see HYLOBATES

GIEMSA STAIN see AZURE STAINS

GIFTED CHILD see CHILD, GIFTED

GIFTS, FINANCIAL see FUND RAISING

GIGANTISM
C5.116.99.492   C5.116.132.479
C19.700.355.528
XR ADENOMA, EOSINOPHILIC
XR GROWTH DISORDERS

GILBERT'S DISEASE see under HYPERBILIRUBINEMIA, HEREDITARY

GILLES DE LA TOURETTE'S DISEASE
C10.228.140.79.450   F3.126.720.894.445
66

GILLS
A13.421
68

GINGIVA
A14.254.646.480
X GUMS

GINGIVAL DISEASES
C7.465.714.258 +
65
X GINGIVOSIS

GINGIVAL EXUDATE see under GINGIVITIS

Fig. 3.5. MeSH alphabetic list.

cross-reference from a term which is not a MeSH heading to one which is, e.g.

 GIEMSA STAIN see AZURE STAINS
 GIFTED CHILD see CHILD, GIFTED

This sort of cross-reference is normally used to guide you from one term to its synonym (alternative word) or to an inverted form of an index phrase.

The second type of cross-reference guides you from a specific term which is not used in MeSH to a broader one which is, e.g.

 GILBERT'S DISEASE see under HYPERBILIRUBINEMIA, HEREDITARY

Gilbert's disease is a condition which is not described much in the literature and if it were a MeSH heading, it is unlikely that many articles would be indexed with it. The user is therefore referred to the broader term, *Hyperbilirubinemia, hereditary,* under which papers on Gilbert's disease would appear in Index Medicus.

The terms in this list are arranged alphabetically and they do not therefore provide an easy guide to their subject relationship. This is obtained from the second half of MeSH, the tree structures, where you will find the same terms listed in a hierarchical subject arrangement in broad categories, such as Urogenital System, Viruses and Nervous System Diseases. The link between the two lists is provided by an alphanumeric code which appears under each full MeSH heading. You will see in Fig. 3.5 that beneath the term GINGIVAL DISEASES there appears the code C7.465.714.258 + and turning to that part of the tree structure we find the MeSH headings listed in Fig. 3.6.

This is part of the larger category C7, which lists all MeSH headings related to diseases of the mouth and tooth. The group of headings shown here relates specifically to periodontal diseases and lists the MeSH headings available (20 in all) to index papers on that subject. So by consulting the tree structures we are able to see all the MeSH headings grouped according to subject and showing their relationship to each other.

What you must also be aware of is that papers which appear in Index Medicus are always indexed under the most specific MeSH heading

PERIODONTAL DISEASES	C7.465.714
GINGIVAL DISEASES	C7.465.714.258
GINGIVAL HEMORRHAGE ·	C7.465.714.258.250
GINGIVAL HYPERPLASIA	C7.465.714.258.267
GINGIVAL HYPERTROPHY	C7.465.714.258.338
GINGIVAL NEOPLASMS	C7.465.714.258.409
GINGIVITIS	C7.465.714.258.480
GINGIVAL EXUDATE ·	C7.465.714.258.480.300
GINGIVAL POCKET ·	C7.465.714.258.480.360
GINGIVITIS, NECROTIZING ULCERATIVE	C7.465.714.258.480.446
GRANULOMA, GIANT CELL	C7.465.714.258.557
PERICORONITIS	C7.465.714.258.771
PERIODONTAL CYST	C7.465.714.470
PERIODONTITIS	C7.465.714.533
PERIODONTAL ABSCESS ·	C7.465.714.533.650
PERIODONTAL POCKET ·	C7.465.714.533.750
PERIODONTOSIS ·	C7.465.714.533.800
TOOTH EXFOLIATION	C7.465.714.773
TOOTH MIGRATION	C7.465.714.836
MESIAL MOVEMENT OF TEETH ·	C7.465.714.836.535
TOOTH MOBILITY	C7.465.714.898
RANULA	C7.465.780
SALIVARY GLAND DISEASES	C7.465.815
MIKULICZ' DISEASE	C7.465.815.355

Fig. 3.6. MeSH tree structure.

available and not under general all-embracing terms. The heading GINGIVAL DISEASES would be used only for general papers on that subject and not for papers dealing with specific diseases of the gingiva. These would be indexed separately under the more specific headings listed. It therefore follows that if you are planning to search through Index Medicus for all papers relating to any diseases of the gingiva you must search under the broad term GINGIVAL DISEASES and also the specific headings listed beneath that term. If you do not do this, you will miss many papers of interest.

This "specificity rule", as it is called, is one of the most important which must be remembered when using Index Medicus. If you do not look in MeSH, and particularly its tree structures, before you use Index Medicus, you can waste a great deal of time searching under incorrect headings and not finding the papers which are there.

One last point should be made about MeSH headings. As you search backwards through Index Medicus (and this is the right way to do it) you may suddenly discover that a heading which you have been using for a number of years no longer appears. The MeSH headings are constantly under review and new headings are regularly introduced to reflect the growth and development of the literature on new subjects. When you are reviewing the literature from the present to the past and your heading "disappears", this is because it is a heading which has only recently been introduced. To find which heading this subject appeared under before the introduction of your term you must turn to the beginning of the Cumulated Index Medicus, where you will find a list of new terms and previously used terms. You can then continue your search under the term which was formerly used to index the subject.

Excerpta Medica

Excerpta Medica, published in the Netherlands, provides abstracts from over 3500 medical and scientific journals, excluding nursing, dentistry and veterinary science. It appears in 43 separate sections, each covering a major medical discipline such as Cancer, Endocrinology and Psychiatry, and each section appears 10 or 12 times a year. Each issue consists of a number of abstracts arranged in broad subject groups followed by an index of authors and subjects.

Figure 3.7 shows an abstract taken from the Gerontology and Geriatrics section and specifically from the subsection relating to the brain and spinal cord. It shows a standard bibliographical reference and provides in addition the address of the authors and an abstract of the paper. To locate this paper in the author index you simply look up the name of any author and this will be followed by the abstract number,

16.1. Brain and spinal cord

1868. Sarcoidosis presenting as senile dementia -
Cordingley G., Navarro C., Brust J.C.M. and Healton
E.B. - Dept. Neurol., Harlem Hosp. Cent., New York,
NY 10037 USA - *NEUROLOGY* 1981 31/9 (1148-1151)

Cerebral sarcoidosis was found at autopsy in a 68-year-old woman with progressive dementia. Of 35 previously reported cases of central nervous system sarcoidosis with dementia, only 1 was over 65 years old, and in only 2 was the presenting clinical syndrome that of a degenerative dementia. Other unusual features of the index case include the restriction of the initial cognitive deficit to memory loss and mild anomia, the scarcity of antemortem evidence for systemic sarcoidosis, a positive tuberculin test, and cerebrospinal fluid (CSF) protein concentration as high as 2028 mg per deciliter. Sarcoidosis is a rare but potentially treatable cause of dementia. Consistently normal CSF probably excludes the diagnosis.

Fig. 3.7. Abstract from Excerpta Medica.

thus enabling you to turn to the main part of Excerpta Medica and find the abstract and complete reference.

The subject index is based not just on the title of the paper but on its content as well and, as Figure 3.8 shows, in this example the indexer has selected four primary indexing terms which indicate the substance of this paper — *sarcoidosis, Alzheimer disease, cerebrospinal fluid* and *dementia*. The index entry is created for each one of these terms which are then followed by the others to give sufficient information for the user to assess the possible value of the article. This paper would, then, appear in the index to this section of Excerpta Medica four times.

sarcoidosis, alzheimer disease, cerebrospinal fluid, dementia, woman of 68, autopsy, 1868
satisfaction, behavior, aging, deprivation, economy, education, conceptual model, campbell, usa, 1945
self concept, aging, doctor patient relation, stereotypy, israel, 1933
self esteem, aged, physical performance, 20 community and 21 institutionalized aged people, ethnic aspects, 1950
  - aged, mental health, social life, 20 community and 21 institutionalized people, 1949
senescence, aging, growth rate, accelerated, aging, biological model, gompertz function, mouse, 1747
senile cataract, aging, cataractogenesis, lens protein, cation, protein, ribonuclease, human lens, 1914
  - adenosine triphosphate, aging, cataract, lens, protein synthesis, 1911
senile dementia, alzheimer disease, astrocyte, brain cortex, histology, fibrous astrocyte, 1892
  - 5 hydroxyindoleacetic acid, alzheimer disease, cerebrospinal fluid, homovanillic acid, 28 cases, 13 controls, 1891

Fig. 3.8. A section of the Excerpta Medica subject index.

After the primary index terms there is also a group of terms which describe the secondary aspects of the paper, in this case, the two entries *woman of 68* and *autopsy*. These two index terms appear at the end of each subject entry, providing extra information about the content of the paper, but will not be index terms in their own right since they do not indicate the major idea of the paper. Again, each entry in the subject index is followed by the abstract number.

The terms used as primary index terms are taken from a thesaurus of 200 000 terms produced by Excerpta Medica known as MALIMET (Master List of Medical Indexing Terms) which is available on computer or microfiche. These are described as "terms under which the editor feels a reader would be most likely to look when searching for that type of article" and so access to this thesaurus is not essential.

Biological Abstracts

With Biological Abstracts the emphasis moves from the literature of clinical medicine towards experimental medicine and the biological sciences. Biological Abstracts, with its companion publication, BA/RRM, which covers reports, reviews and meetings, presents us with abstracts from more than 9000 journals, plus books, monographs and conference proceedings, and can with justification describe itself as the world's largest collection of abstracts and citations for biology in the English language. It appears fortnightly and each issue consists of abstracts arranged in very broad subject groups such as Enzymes, Muscle and Radiation Biology. Figure 3.9 shows an abstract from the references relating to the digestive system. This takes the form of a standard bibliographical reference and also includes the authors' address and an abstract of the paper. The references in each volume are numbered consecutively and this facilitates their retrieval when they have been located in the indexes.

There are five indexes in all. The first is the author index, which is simply an alphabetical list of the names of the authors of all abstracts contained in each issue. Each name is followed by the abstract number. The Biosystematic Index is used to find abstracts by taxonomic categories; the Generic Index is used to trace abstracts according to genus-species name; and the Concept Index is used to find abstracts relating to broad subject areas like ecology, microbiology and toxicology. These three require a little practice but once you are used to using them they can be helpful. Each issue of Biological Abstracts contains clear instructions on their use. The final index is the Subject Index and this is the most useful of all. Unlike the indexes to the two previous publications, this is not compiled from an authoritative list of terms but is computer-generated from all the significant words, known as keywords, in the

8828. FLYNN, JOHN T.*, JOSEPH M. HENRY and SANDRA PERKOWSKI. (Dep. Physiology, Jefferson Med. College, 1020 Locust St., Philadelphia, Pa. 19107.) CAN J PHYSIOL PHARMACOL 59(12): 1268-1273. 1981[recd. 1982]. [In Engl. with Engl. and Fr. summ.] **Phospholipase A2 stimulated release of prostanoids from the isolated, perfused rabbit liver: Implications in regional cellular injury.**—A direct relationship between the activity of the arachidonic acid cascade in vivo and the extent of cellular damage following several types of experimental injury was previously demonstrated. Since phospholipase activity has been shown to regulate arachidonic acid availability, the ability of circulating phospholipase A2 (PLA2) of pancreatic origin to stimulate prostanoid production or induce cellular injury in the isolated, perfused rabbit liver was tested. Experimental conditions were similar to those present during pancreatitis or early splanchnic artery occlusion shock. The administration of PLA2 at a rate of 100 U/min for 10 min resulted in enhanced rates of thromboxane B2 and 6-ketoprostaglandin F1α release between 1-5 min into the infusion period. No changes in hepatic perfusion pressure, vascular resistance, wet tissue weight or release of lactic dehydrogenase or acid phosphatase into the effluent were observed in vehicle or PLA2-treated livers. Cellular injury was not a factor in the prostanoid release. Circulating PLA2 can apparently directly stimulate de novo prostanoid synthesis in noninjured tissues. Enhanced plasma prostanoid concentrations in intact animals during periods of regional cellular injury may be due in part to circulating PLA2 released from damaged tissues.

Fig. 3.9. Extract from Biological Abstracts.

paper's title together with others which may be added by the editorial staff of Biological Abstracts when the title is not considered to be sufficiently informative.

To use this index you simply look up a word in the keyword column of the Subject Index and there you will find all the papers which have that word in their titles, together with a portion of the title on either side of this keyword to enable you to assess the relevance of the paper.

Figure 3.10 shows how the paper we have already seen would appear in the Subject Index under the keyword *prostanoids*. To the right of the title you see the reference number 63308, which enables you to go to the main section of Biological Abstracts and read the abstracts in full. Similar entries for the same title will be found in the Subject Index under every keyword in the title.

Before you start to search this index you should compile a list of keywords likely to be of interest to you. Always remember that since this is produced from the titles of papers, you need to think of every possible word that an author may have used and that if you forget any you may miss an important paper. Remember too that you must search for plural forms of words, synonyms and adjectival forms. One other point to bear in mind is that since keywords are listed strictly in alphabetical order, singular forms of nouns may be separated from plural forms by many other words; the word "horse", for example, will be separated from its plural by a large number of titles containing the word "horseradish".

This type of index is known as a KWIC index (Keyword in context) and is one that is frequently encountered in scientific indexing journals.

```
       MENT OF !3 THIA    PROSTANOIDS  /SYNTHESIS AND REARRA    63308
  OGENOUS FORMATION OF                 AND THE LEVELS OF LONG   45221
 CIAL REFERENCE TO THE                 AS METABOLIC AGENTS IN   73701
 IN-VITRO PRODUCTION OF                BY CULTURED BOVINE ART   31184
 STIMULATED RELEASE OF                 FROM THE ISOLATED PERF    8828
 RDIAL ISCHEMIA IN DOGS                PULMONARY ARTERIAL PR    22898
 ENTION SEPTUM DIVISION  PROSTATE  /CONGENITAL PATENT URACH     72843
 DYMIS SEMINAL VESICLES            /EFFECT OF GERIFORTE ON M    70885
 ISSION FACTOR BLADDER             /FURTHER EXPERIENCES WITH    21756
 CELL CARCINOMA OF THE             A CASE HUMAN PICIBANIL IM    26180
 MENT/ ADENOSIS OF THE             A DYSPLASTIC LESION THAT C    4134
 LAND MAMMARY GLAND                ADENO CARCINOMA CANALICU     11332
```

Fig. 3.10. A section of the Biological Abstracts subject index.

Although it may seem difficult to use at first, once you have mastered the principle it can be a very effective means of searching the literature with a high degree of specificity.

Science Citation Index

Science Citation Index differs from other indexes and introduces us to the concept of citation indexing. Before we look at Science Citation Index it will be useful first to understand the principle of citation indexing. As you will soon discover when reading the scientific literature, most papers have a list of references at the end which provide further reading. These references may be listed to substantiate a statement made in the text, to show the original description of a method used or to point out other papers on the same subject. Whatever their purpose, there is a direct subject relationship between the paper you are reading and those it cites. Many readers will refer to these earlier papers for more information. Science Citation Index quite simply enables this process to be reversed, that is, the reader is able to take an early reference which he knows to be of interest and to locate later papers which have cited it.

Science Citation Index now appears six times a year with an annual cumulation and consists of three separate but related indexes: the Citation Index, the Source Index, and the Permuterm Subject Index. The best way to understand the function of these and the method of using Science Citation Index is to follow through an actual example (Fig. 3.11a–e).

Let us assume that we have come across a reference which is not only interesting but is one to be regarded as a key paper on the subject. We are therefore interested in tracing any papers that have cited it since it was first published. The key reference used as an example is shown in Fig. 3.11a.

We first turn to the latest available issue of the Citation Index, where we find an alphabetical list, by first author's name, of all the papers cited in the period covered by the index. Under each name the cited papers are listed in chronological order and we find that the second paper under K.L. Casey's name is the one we want (Fig. 3.11b). (Note that the journal reference only is given; the title of the paper is not necessary.) From this we learn that the paper by Casey has been cited by D. Mitchell in Proceedings of the Royal Society, Series B, 1977, *197*, p.169. At this point we may go straight to the citing reference in the Proceedings . . . or, if this journal is not immediately available, we turn to another section of Science Citation Index, the Source Index.

Figure 3.11c shows part of the Source Index, which is an alphabetical list by author of all the citing papers appearing in the journals covered.

Casey KL: Unit analysis of nociceptive mechanisms in the thalamus of the awake squirrel monkey.
J Neurophysiol 29:727-50, Jul 66

Fig 3.11a. Key reference.

CASEY KL
61 J PHYSIOL LOND 158 399
    PERCIAVA V   BRAIN RES   N   126   551 77
66 J NEUROPHYSIOL   29   727
    MITCHELL D   P ROY SOC B   191   169 77
67 NEW CONCEPTS PAIN IT   13
    PAGNI CA   BK # 00587   R   1977   132 77
69 BRAIN RES   13   155
    THOREN P   J APP PHYSL   42   461 77
69 EXP NEUROL   25   35
    SHIMA K   FOL PHARM J   73   135 77
71 SCIENCE   173   77
    SIEGEL JM   SCIENCE   196   678 77
73 AM SCI   61   194
    SITARAM N   EUR J PHARM   42   285 77
73 BRAIN UNIT ACTIVITY   115
    KEENE JJ   BRAIN RES B   1   517 76
74 ADV NEUROLOGY   4   197
    KEENE JJ   BEHAV BIOL   N   19   527 77
    PAGNI CA   BK # 00587   R   1977   132 77

Fig. 3.11b. Key reference.

MITCHELL CW
  see YONOVITZ A   J ACOUST SO   '61 S 4 77
MITCHELL D
  SCOTT DW MITCHELL LN—ATTENUATED AND ENHANCED
  NEOPHOBIA IN TASTE-AVERSION DELAY OF
  REINFORCEMENT EFFECT
ANIM LEAR B 5(1):99-102   77   19R
    UNIV WASHINGTON, SEATTLE, WA 98195, USA
  FAIRBANK M LAYCOCK JD—SUPPRESSION OF NEOPHOBIA
  BY CHLORPROMAZINE IN WILD RATS
BEHAV BIOL   19(3):309-323   77   36R
    UNIV WASHINGTON,DEPT PSYCHOL, SEATTLE, WA 98195,
    USA
  PARKER DG—DIFFERING STATE STANDARDS AND WASTE
  TREATMENT COST
J ENVIR ENG   103(3):389-396   77   8R
    UNIV ARKANSAS, FAYETTEVILLE, AR 72701, USA
  HELLON RF—NEURONAL AND BEHAVIORAL-RESPONSES IN
  RATS DURING NOXIOUS-STIMULATION OF TAIL
P ROY SOC B   197(1127):169-194   77   76R
    NATL INST MED RES, LONDON NW7 1AA, ENGLAND
  see LABURN H   J PHYSL LON   267   559 77
  see WILTSHAW E   BR MED J   1 1214 77
MITCHELL DC
  see MISHRA SC   J MED EN TE   1   159 77
MITCHELL DE

Fig. 3.11c. Relevant part of the Source Index.

Proc. R. Soc. Lond. B. **197**, 169–194 (1977)
Printed in Great Britain

Neuronal and behavioural responses in rats during noxious stimulation of the tail

By D. Mitchell† and R. F. Hellon

National Institute for Medical Research, Mill Hill, London NW7 1AA

(Communicated by Sir Arnold Burgen, F.R.S. – Received 8 April 1976)

Burgess, P. R. 1974 The physiology of pain. Am. J. Chin. Med. **2**, 121–148.
Carroll, M. N. & Lim, R. K. S. 1960 Observations on the neuropharmacology of morphine and morphinelike analgesia. Arch. int. Pharmacodyn. **125**, 383–403.
Casey, K. L. 1966 Unit analysis of nociceptive mechanisms in the thalamus of the awake squirrel monkey. J. Neurophysiol. **29**, 727–750.
Cervero, F., Iggo, & Ogawa, H. 1976 Nociceptive-driven dorsal horn neurones in the lumbar spinal cord of the cat. Pain **2**, 5–24.

Fig. 3.11d. Part of the article itself.

NOXIOUS-STIMULATI.
  BEHAVIORAL ●MITCHELL D
  CHEMICAL   - -●MENSE S
  FOLLOWING -
  NERVOUS   - -
  NEURONAL   - MITCHELL D
  NEURONS   - -●CERVERO F
  OUTFLOW - - MENSE S
  RATS - - - - MITCHELL D
  REACTION-T -●SHIOMI K
  RESPONSES - CERVERO F
  SKELETAL-M MENSE S
  SKIN - - - - CERVERO F
  SPINOCERVI -
  TAIL - - - - MITCHELL D
  THRESHOLD - SHIOMI K
  TRACT - - - CERVERO F

Fig. 3.11e. Relevant part of the Permuterm Subject Index.

Under Mitchell D. we have a list of papers written by him and find towards the end the one we are looking for. We now know that it was written jointly with R. F. Hellon and its title is "Neuronal and behavioural responses in rats during noxious stimulation of tail". The full journal reference is given again and the R after the page number gives us the additional information that this new paper is a review.

If we now look at the article itself (Fig. 3.11d) we find at the end a list of 80 references, among which is our original paper by Casey which started the search off. So, by checking through just one issue of Science Citation Index we have found one paper which has not only cited our key paper but many others too, a number of which will probably be of interest to us. If we want even more references we can continue the search through the Citation Index in reverse date order until we have accumulated enough. We cannot, of course, extend the search earlier than the publication date of the orginal reference.

Although the main purpose of Science Citation Index is to search the literature through citations, its compilation, which is by computer, has facilitated the production of a new index known as the Permuterm Subject Index. In the Permuterm Subject Index every significant word or word phrase from the titles of the citing papers is paired with every other significant word in the same title. These pairs are printed out and are followed by the author's name, thereby providing us with a subject approach to the journals covered by Science Citation Index. To take the example of the paper by Mitchell, we see (Fig. 3.11e) under the word phrase "noxious stimulation" (space does not permit the complete phrase to be printed) all the other important words in the title, and each leads us to the name D. Mitchell. Checking this name in the Source Index as before would give us the complete reference to Mitchell's paper.

One other way in which Science Citation Index differs from other indexing journals is that it is interdisciplinary. It aims to cover the whole field of science and its selection of journals is based on the number of times papers in these journals are actually cited by later writers. It is particularly useful as a supplement to other indexes in subject areas where terminology is vague but a key reference is known and also in areas where the literature is scattered among many scientific disciplines.

Comparison of Indexes

The above four indexing and abstracting services are the most comprehensive in the life sciences. Is any one better than the others? How many of them should you search through? Which is the most suitable to use for your particular search? Are there any others which could usefully be searched? This section aims to answer some of these questions.

The first criterion which will affect your selection of an index will be the subject. If your interest is primarily in the field of clinical medicine, the main choice is between Index Medicus and Excerpta Medica.

Index Medicus is probably the easier to use for retrospective searches. As you work backwards from the current monthly issue you will soon come to annual cumulations for earlier years and this makes the task much simpler because all the references which previously appeared in the monthly issues are now cumulated in several large volumes but in one alphabetical sequence. Index Medicus is also physically easier to use because under each MeSH heading is a list of complete references which you can note instantly and consult later. The main problem is understanding the MeSH headings. It is too easy to bypass this stage and go straight into the index itself without having first checked on the most suitable headings to look for. If you make a mistake about the headings you can waste a lot of time looking through Index Medicus with no result.

Excerpta Medica's principal advantage over Index Medicus is that it has a much greater coverage, indexing 3500 journals plus an unspecified number of books, conference papers and dissertations. Since it lists its papers in a classified order it is convenient for keeping up to date, although this arrangement is not so useful for retrospective searching. The indexes cumulate in each volume but the abstracts do not, so that to search through a bound volume you first need to consult the index, make a note of all the abstract numbers that seem useful and then turn to each one of these individually. This is more time consuming than the corresponding process in Index Medicus. The subject index in Excerpta Medica is compiled from over 200 000 terms as opposed to the 14 000 MeSH headings, which permits the indexing of papers to be much more specific. Although there is an overlap in the coverage of the two, Excerpta Medica does not include paramedical subjects in any detail but is particularly strong and aims for completeness in the area of drugs and potential drugs and must be first choice in that field. In addition to providing a standard bibliographical reference, Excerpta Medica also provides a well-written informative abstract of the paper and gives the address of the author so that you can write for a reprint.

In short, each of these two indexes has its advantages and its snags. It is not easy to give guidelines as to which is the better. Your choice can only come from experience and you will eventually settle for the one you are happier using.

If your interest is less directed towards clinical medicine and more towards experimental medicine and the life sciences, then *Biological Abstracts* is your first choice, and indeed it has no comparable rivals. Of its many indexes the one which you are most likely to use is its subject index and you must understand how it is produced and become familiar with it as quickly as possible. The golden rule is to think of every possible word that an author could have used in the title of a paper and to search under every one of these, together with their plural and adjectival forms. Even in clinical medicine Biological Abstracts will probably produce papers not found in either Excerpta Medica or Index Medicus, but unless your retrieval from either of these is particularly small or unless you want as complete a coverage as possible, the extra effort in searching Biological Abstracts is probably not worthwhile.

As we have seen, *Science Citation Index* differs in its methods of indexing and two occasions stand out when it should be the most useful index for you. First, when the indexing terms in the others are not specific enough to cover the topic and you already know a key paper in the subject. Secondly, when your subject overlaps with several scientific disciplines such as medical physics or biomedical engineering.

Two other major indexes on the periphery of the life sciences deserve a brief mention at this point as they may prove useful in certain circumstances. The first is *Psychological Abstracts*. This is smaller than any of the indexes previously described, covering approximately 1000 journals and 1500 monographs a year. In appearance it is rather like Excerpta Medica and is a very valuable source of information in psychology, psychiatry and related behavioural sciences, including anthropology, linguistics and pharmacology.

The other is *Chemical Abstracts,* an enormous publication, producing abstracts from over 12 000 journals and 1000 books a year. Although much of its content relates to pure chemistry and is unlikely to be of interest to workers in the life sciences, it does provide good coverage and give extra information in related areas such as biochemistry, toxicology, immunochemistry and pharmacology.

Specialist Indexing Journals

In addition to the major indexes and abstracts there are a large number of indexes which cover a narrower subject area. These include such titles as Artificial Kidney Bibliography, Biological Membrane Abstracts, and Carcinogenesis Abstracts.

These specialist indexing journals can offer a number of advantages that the larger ones do not possess. Their smaller size often means that they are less expensive and can be purchased for use in laboratories or by individuals; this also applies to the sections of Excerpta Medica which can be bought separately. Because they set out to cover a well-defined subject area in great detail, they tend to acquire their references from all available sources and not just from a pre-planned list of journals. Since they are produced for specialists they are often able to index in greater depth and with greater specificity than are the larger indexes.

A specialist indexing journal, if available, should always be consulted in addition to one of the major indexes. You will invariably find that it will produce additional references previously unknown to you. Various lists of indexes and abstracts are available. The most comprehensive and most up-to-date can be found at the beginning of the current edition of *Ulrich's International Periodicals Directory,* which can be consulted in most libraries.

Reviews

Most indexing and abstracting journals set out to index the entire contents of the journals they cover with the exception, perhaps, of letters, news items and brief communications. No attempt, however, is made to assess the quality of the papers indexed; all are treated equally.

For a more selective approach to the literature you need recourse to a review paper. Such papers are usually written by an expert who surveys and critically analyses the literature of a subject over a specific period of time. They invariably carry personal evaluation from the author and have a good list of recommended references, and are therefore an excellent starting point for anyone unfamiliar with the literature in that field. Review papers appear most commonly in journals specifically designed for the purpose. They are usually identifiable from their titles, which begin with words such as "*Yearbook* of . . .", "*Recent Advances* in . . ." and "*Annual Review* of . . .", and together they constitute a very valuable collection of surveys of the literature. Occasionally journals which carry conventional papers will also publish a commissioned review as a special feature.

It is estimated that only 3% or 4% of the total scientific literature consists of review papers, and although many indexing and abstracting journals usually indicate them in some way, looking for them can be inefficient and time consuming. There are, fortunately, two indexing journals which index only review papers. The *Bibliography of Medical Reviews* appears as part of Index Medicus. The *Index to Scientific Reviews* is a separate publication which contains only those reviews which have appeared in Science Citation Index. Both are used in the same way as their parent index and should always be consulted first when a review paper is wanted.

Computer Searching

In most cases a hand search through the most appropriate indexing or abstracting journal will be sufficient to produce a number of suitable references for you. However, the development of computers and particularly their application to the production of indexes has added a new and exciting dimension to literature searching and has made it easy to search on subjects which were previously very difficult, if not impossible, to deal with manually. All the publications just described, and very many others, can now be searched online by computer. Terminals to access these databases, as they are called, can now be found in many medical, hospital and academic libraries. There are also librarians with special skills in computer searching who are able to advise on search formulations and perform searches for their readers.

Although computer searching can be used for even the simplest requests, such as locating references on the aetiology of diabetes, it then does little more than reproduce the same references as in the printed index and has no advantage over hand searching save that of time. The occasions on which computer searching really does have advantages are too numerous to describe in detail here, but basically the more complex or more specific the information being sought, the more beneficial a computer search is likely to be.

To give some idea of how computer searching works, let us look at a fairly typical complex search which would not be easy to do by hand. Let us assume that you are looking for references on the effects of lead on the nervous system of pre-school children. For any reference to be of interest to you it would have to mention each of the three concepts — lead, nervous system and pre-school child. These are very precise and such a search lends itself easily to computer methods.

The first step is to discuss your needs with your librarian, who would recommend the most suitable database; in this case it would almost certainly be Excerpta Medica, Index Medicus (known in its computerised version as Medline) and Psychological Abstracts. You would then together compile a list of the most appropriate words or phrases which best describe the required concepts. These could be selected either from a thesaurus used in the database (e.g. MeSH on Medline) or simply from words which might be expected to appear in the titles of relevant papers. After these preliminary preparations, the librarian would access the computer holding the database and the search would take place. The progress of the search, which in this example is based on Medline, is shown in Figure 3.12.

The user first enters the terms "Lead" and "Lead poisoning" and the computer indicates that there are 1126 references containing these terms on its database. It stores them as set number 1, and will retain them in its memory until the user issues further instructions. The same procedure

```
SS 1 /C?
USER:
LEAD OR LEAD POISONING
PROG:
SS (1) PSTG (1126)

SS 2 /C?
USER:
NERVOUS SYSTEM
PROG:
SS (2) PSTG (63061)

SS 3 /C?
USER:
CHILD, PRESCHOOL
PROG:
SS (3) PSTG (35420)

SS 4 /C?
USER:
1 AND 2 AND 3
PROG:
SS (4) PSTG (3)

SS 5 /C?
USER:
PRINT
PROG:

1
AU  - Bryce-Smith D ; Stephens R
TI  - Led and brain function [letter]
SO  - Dev Med Child Neurol 1982 Feb;24(1):90-1

2
AU  - Benignus VA ; Otto DA ; Muller KE ; Seiple KJ
TI  - Effects of age and body lead burden on CNS function in young
      children. II. EEG spectra.
SO  - Electroencephalogr Clin Neurophysiol 1981 Oct;52(4):240-8

3
AU  - Otto DA ; Benignus VA ; Muller KE ; Barton CN
TI  - Effects of age and body lead burden on CNS function in young
      children. I. slow cortical potentials.
SO  - Electroencephalogr Clin Neurophysiol 1981 Oct;52(4):229-39
```

Fig. 3.12. Medline search.

takes place to create similar sets of references on "Nervous system" and "Pre-school child". The computer has stored three separate sets of references and what the user now needs to know is how many appear in all three sets — in other words, how many contain all three concepts. To do this he asks for all sets to be combined and the computer does so, indicating that this new set (Number 4) contains three references. These are printed online immediately, giving the enquirer the complete bibliographical citation for each one; a larger number of references would usually be printed offline and sent to the user by post. It is interesting to note that although the word "lead" in the first reference has been misspelt both on Medline and in Index Medicus, the paper has been successfully retrieved because the MeSH heading was spelt correctly.

This example shows how, in under 5 minutes, several years of the literature can be scanned and, from the 1126 references on lead, only those dealing specifically with its effect on the nervous system of the preschool child have been located and printed out.

A charge is often made for computer searches although this depends on the policy of the institution concerned. It is, however, always worth remembering that any cost should be offset against a considerable amount of time saved and the probability that a more efficient search has been performed. There are now over three hundred databases which may be searched online. Your librarian will be able to show you a complete list together with full details of their subject coverage. A selection of those most frequently used in the life sciences is given in Table 3.1.

In addition to its value in retrospective searching, the computer can be especially useful in the production of current awareness services to match exactly the user's needs. The procedure for organising such a search is simple. The user and librarian together select the database most likely to produce relevant references and produce a search profile as was done above. This is stored in the computer and as the database is updated with new references, usually at monthly intervals, those which match this profile will be printed out and automatically sent to the user. The main advantage of such a service is that it alerts the user to references he would not have come across because they appear in journals he does not normally read. A further advantage is that such searches are often able to produce references several weeks before they appear in the printed index from which they are taken.

Other Sources of Information

The sources described so far index mainly the contents of journals. Some occasionally index conference proceedings and monographs but they

Table 3.1 A select list of databases which may be searched online

Database	Subject coverage
Agricola	Agriculture and related subjects
BIOSIS	All life sciences, including experimental medicine
CAB Abstracts	Agriculture, horticulture, animal breeding, dairy science, veterinary science etc.
Chemical Abstracts	All aspects of chemistry
Enviroline	Environmental studies
Excerpta Medica	Medicine, excluding nursing, dentistry and veterinary medicine
Health	Non-clinical aspects of health care, including administration, finance and legislation
IPA	Pharmacy and the development and use of drugs
Life Sciences Collection	Animal behaviour, ecology, entomology, genetics etc.
Medline	All aspects of medicine, including nursing and dentistry
Pollution Abstracts	Environmentally related literature on pollution and its control
Population Bibliography	Demography, abortion, fertility studies and population research
Psycinfo	Psychology and related behavioural and social sciences
Scisearch	A multidisciplinary index derived from the Science Citation Index
Toxline	Human and animal toxicology, adverse drug reactions environmental pollution

should not be regarded as the sole source of information for non-journal literature.

Although they do not perform the same function as journals, it can on occasion be useful to have a list of books on a subject to provide background reading. A number of publications exist to provide this information. There are three main types of publication giving details of books — those listing titles currently in print, national bibliographies and catalogues of large libraries.

The first group consists of volumes published annually with titles like Books in Print, British Books in Print and Canadian Books in Print, which provide a useful quick list of books currently available. They usually have lists according to authors, titles and subjects and provide full bibliographical details of books so that they may be easily traced in a library.

National bibliographies serve primarily as an official list of books published in one particular country or geographical area. They usually deal with all subjects and do not cumulate so that it is necessary to search through such publications in each year separately. They are, nevertheless, a good source and can produce as complete a list as is possible of books published within a country. Examples of national bibliographies are British National Bibliography, Bibliografía Mexicana and Australian National Bibliography.

Probably the most convenient way to acquire a list of publications on a subject is to check the catalogue of a large library, especially if it is considered to have a good collection in that subject. Although even the largest libraries cannot be comprehensive in their stock, very little of significance tends to escape them. Large libraries with published catalogues are the British Museum, the Library of Congress and the Bibliothèque Nationale. Libraries with special collections which have published catalogues include the London School of Hygiene and Tropical Medicine, the Wellcome Institute for the History of Medicine, and the largest medical library in the world, the National Library of Medicine in the U.S.A.

Two other categories of literature which must be mentioned are *theses* and *conference proceedings.* It is important not to overlook these since they often contain the results of important research which may not appear elsewhere. Furthermore, because they are not published in the conventional way, they do not always appear in any of the bibliographies mentioned above. Separate guides exist for both. Dissertation Abstracts International provides full details, including an abstract, of theses accepted in American and many European universities. This publication is produced by an American organisation, University Microfilms, which makes microfilm copies of all theses which are then available for purchase. This is the most comprehensive index of theses currently available but many countries produce their own national lists, such as Canadian Theses and Index of Theses Accepted for Higher Degrees by the Universities of Great Britain and Ireland.

The most valuable guide to conferences is Proceedings in Print, which covers proceedings of a broad range of meetings, including seminars, colloquia etc., in all languages. Most of the sources described will be available in libraries of a medium size.

Language Problems

The indexes and abstracts that have been described are all published in English from English-speaking countries and all assume a reading knowledge of English among their users as instructions and index terms are all given in English. This does not mean that material in languages other than English are excluded; indeed, they all cover literature from other countries to a varying extent, usually, as we have seen, translating the titles of papers into English.

The exclusion of "non-English" indexes does not reflect chauvinism on the part of the writer but rather indicates the true state of scientific literature today. English is the lingua franca of scientific communication and all researchers working in the international arena must have at least a reading knowledge of it. Most indexes are extremely expensive to produce and it is unlikely that a large market would be available for any published in other languages. A number of national indexes appear, such as the Bibliografia Brasileira de Medicina and the Magyar Orvosi Bibliographia, but these can be of little use outside their countries of origin. Two foreign language indexes which should be mentioned because of their wider coverage are the French Bulletin Signalétique and the Russian Referativnyi Zhurnal.

This is an appropriate place to give a brief mention to translation services. Many libraries hold lists of names of professional translators and published lists are also available. It must be pointed out, however, that obtaining a translation is not cheap. This is not surprising since a well qualified translator should not only be fluent in several languages but should also have a reasonable knowledge of the subject matter of the paper he is translating. Such expertise is not easy to come by and when found it demands proper recompense.

Keeping up to Date

The guidelines described so far all enable a retrospective search of the literature to be undertaken. However, while you are working on your own research, papers will continue to be published and you will find it a problem trying to keep up to date. No doubt you will be subscribing to copies of any general or specialist journals that are needed and it is important to make a regular practice of scanning journals on the library shelf and to take other steps to keep abreast of what is being published.

Although you can check through each issue of the indexing journal of your choice, these large indexes are designed primarily for retrospective searching and do not lend themselves easily to current awareness. One publication which does do this is Current Contents. This is published weekly in seven editions (Clinical Practice; Agriculture, Biology and Environmental Sciences; Engineering, Technology and Applied Sciences; Social and Behavioral Sciences; Life Sciences; Physical, Chemical and Earth Sciences; Arts and Humanities) which reproduce the contents pages of the most important journals in their respective fields. Each issue also contains a subject index of the papers in each journal and an index of authors together with their addresses, which facilitates the acquisition of reprints.

Current Contents can be used most profitably in three ways. By looking through the author index for names of authors you know to be working in your field of interest, you can easily keep up with their publications. You can also follow up journals which usually contain interesting papers. A list of journals indexed is published at the front of each issue and if any of yours are included, the complete contents list will appear in Current Contents even though the journal itself may not be accessible to you. Lastly, the *Subject Index,* which is similar to the *Permuterm Subject Index* of *Science Citation Index,* gives you a subject approach to the literature.

For those who do not have easy access to a library or are unable to wait for an author's reprint, there is a service unique to Current Contents known as *Original Article Text Service,* whereby for a fee the original paper is removed from its parent journal and mailed direct to the requester (Fig. 3.13).

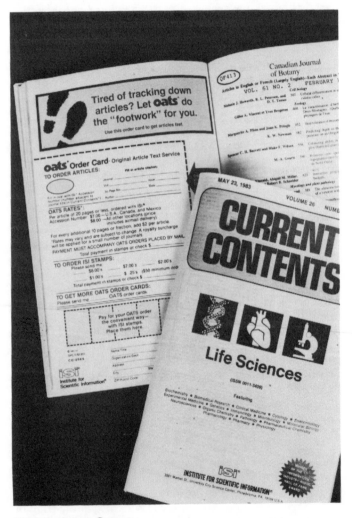

Fig. 3.13. Current Contents.

The principal advantages of such services are their frequency of publication and the speed at which papers appear, often anticipating their listing in a conventional index by several months. They do, however, require a determined effort on the part of the user to scan each issue regularly to collect all references likely to be of value. Aware of this, the Institute of Scientific Information, publishers of Current Contents, now issue over 400 specialised reading lists devoted to one particular specialised subject, e.g. antihypertensive agents, cancer immunology. Known as ASCATOPICS, these appear weekly, are available on subscription and list all pertinent references from nearly 5000 journals.

Probably the most useful alerting service is one tailored exactly to the user's research interest. The method of organising this using computer information retrieval methods was described earlier.

Conclusion

It cannot be denied that the process of literature searching is time consuming and laborious. It is, however, an essential preliminary step which must be taken in research work and one which should not be overlooked. As we have seen, many guides exist to help you; computer retrieval services can be particularly valuable, and advice is always available from colleagues or library staff. It is tempting to bypass a literature search and begin at once on the more exciting and rewarding aspects of your work, but many have later realised the folly of this upon discovering too late that the same work has been previously published elsewhere. This is an unfortunate situation which can and should be avoided. Your principal purpose is to establish by searching the literature that you are doing something new, to carry out your planned research project and to publish the results. Remember that in this final step, that of publishing, you will not only be communicating the results of your work to the scientific world but also adding to the ever-increasing scientific literature which will have to be searched by those who come after you.

4 Speaking at Meetings

Clifford Hawkins

Begin with an arresting sentence; close with a strong summary; in between speak simply, clearly and always to the point; and above all be brief.

William J. Mayo[1] (1861–1939)

Speaking at meetings is a quicker way of reporting work than writing articles. Unfortunately, as the number of medical meetings increases, the communications delivered become harder to understand. There are several reasons for this. Formerly the contents of papers often consisted of brief descriptions of clinical or pathological conditions, whereas today scientific papers may occupy an entire session. Greater care is then demanded from the speaker and sometimes more intelligence from his audience. Priority is given to research. Also, the trend towards specialisation — each speciality with its own jargon and terminology — creates problems in intercommunication. One sometimes wonders whether general meetings will not soon become impracticable. Nevertheless, none of these developments should prevent a communication being understood, provided that it is properly delivered. Sometimes in a meeting lasting many hours, one communication only may be conspicuous for its clarity and fine slides — its presentation so concise and easy that few appreciate the work that went into its construction.

The thought of talking in public is alarming even to the experienced. Giving a communication at a medical meeting is no exception. Indeed, there are other worries apart from having to face an audience. For example, the strict time limit which may be 10 or 15 minutes; into this the speaker has, or rather imagines he has, to pack the results of research over months or years. It is not surprising that some communications are incomprehensible. However, it is possible to make complex matters comprehensible to all the audience. Sometimes a speaker may give a paper, but no one, not even the erudite, understands him. You meet the speaker in the corridor and he will tell you clearly in 1 or 2 minutes what his work is about. The reason for his failure on the podium is that he has either not prepared his talk or piles up every fragment of evidence to

---

1. Quoted by Helen Clapesattle (1941) The doctors Mayo. University of Minnesota Press

prove his case and merely succeeds in confusing. It is only possible to make three or four points and these must be clearly in mind.

Differences Between Speaking and Writing

Speaking is an art by itself. The temptation to use an article perhaps already in the press as text for a talk should be resisted. It is better to plan the communication anew. A speech should be looser in texture, and less detailed, than an article. A reader chooses his own pace, lingering over obscure passages or skipping quickly over pieces of less interest and importance — or he can put down a book and come back to it when he has learned more. The listener, by contrast, must accept the speed chosen by the speaker. An annoyed or antagonised listener will in spirit leave you and as far as your talk is concerned, he will never come back. In listening, continuous attention is needed; there is no time to pause, to linger over difficult passages, or to study an illustration again. One unknown word which makes the listener stumble, and think, may cause loss of contact with the speaker. So the speaker must speak clearly and simply, indicating when he is moving on to the next point — for the listener does not have ideas separated by punctuation or paragraphs — and perhaps repeating key points. No one wants to hear a speaker "talking like a book".

Planning a Communication

Some speakers have a natural ability to make an interesting subject dull or a simple one complicated; others can imbue a complicated subject with an interest and clarity which captivates their audience. It is generally true that the clearer the delivery, the harder the work that has been put into its preparation (Fig. 4.1). The person who boasts that he has thought out his talk in the train on the way to the meeting may sometimes be brilliant; more often the listener will wish that the journey had been longer or not undertaken at all.

Form and Style

The simple pattern — beginning, middle and end — should be followed. A short introduction is not only desirable for clarity but also a natural courtesy to those unfamiliar with the subject; and there is seldom an

```
┌─────────────────────────────┐
│                             │
│   Preparation               │
│   Pruning                   │
│   Rehearsal                 │
│                             │
└─────────────────────────────┘
```

Fig. 4.1. Three essentials for good communication.

audience so specialised as not to appreciate this. An opening such as "May I have the lights out, first slide please" should be avoided. Too long introductions can also be irritating, especially when repeating the same theme, for example, when the conference concerns a single subject.

The material itself may consist of work that has taken one or more years and it is impossible to condense this into minutes. The purpose of the talk — to bring out the three or more points that can be made in the allotted time — should therefore be clearly in mind. "The overwhelming itch to insert every possible detail, lest a sharp-shooting critic may cavil, will destroy the artistic quality", as an editorial aptly put it (Editorial 1964). Strict pruning of unnecessary or complex data is essential. All material should be scrutinised to find the best way of showing it, whether by graph, histogram or diagram. Columns of figures and tables are often best converted into bar charts or diagrams showing relationships and trends. It is the idea derived from the data rather than the figures themselves that are the point. Details, such as tables, list of figures and experimental methods, can be available afterwards to anyone interested.

Every communication given at a general meeting should be viewed as a challenge to bridge the gap between specialities. The aim should be the average person in the audience, not the specialist or superspecialist, and the simplest member of the audience should be able to understand. There is a story in one learned society that when young inexperienced research workers come to give a talk, they are warned "remember you are addressing a most distinguished assembly of scientists. Therefore, you should speak to them as though they are children of four years of age". Slight hyperbole perhaps but it is a pity that more speakers do not follow this guide. Any fool can make things sound complicated; it is the clever person whose audience all understand the talk.

The language, whenever possible, should be in plain English, not jargon. Short words of Anglo-Saxon origin have a force and clarity often lacking in polysyllabic words from Latin or Greek. The golden rule of writing, said Gowers (1973), lies in the choice of words and this applies as much to speaking. Even when the address is fully prepared and rehearsed it is a pleasant and useful exercise to look through it with dictionary or reference book at hand, finding better words, and eliminating clichés and words which through constant use have ceased to convey any meaning to the hearer.

Humour gives flavour to a talk and can be used to reinforce serious ideas. It also provides light relief from complex subjects and revives interest, though to use it successfully is an art. Humour must be really good; for a puny or distasteful attempt to be funny will detract from the quality of the lecture and embarrass the audience.

The conclusion should be as clear as the introduction, an emphasis on main points or a suggestion for final thought. Incomplete work is often more interesting than completed work and the talk may end with the idea "where do I go from here?" or the speaker himself may speculate about future developments in the subject discussed. The audience should know clearly when the end of the talk has been reached and may indeed be pleased to know this. The words "finally" or "in conclusion" can be used but listeners are antagonised when these are used several times and the speaker is still there on his feet talking.

Timing

A speaker who exceeds his allotted time without permission from the Chair may upset the entire plan of a meeting, for time may have to be stolen from other speakers or discussion curtailed. Reputations have been spoiled by speaking for too long. The shorter the paper, the more popular the speaker. Much care should therefore be given to this, and it is better to aim at 1 or 2 minutes less than the full time allowed. It is difficult to estimate the time needed for showing slides, and the projectionist may meet difficulties with his machine. Time spent drawing on a blackboard or overhead projector is notoriously unpredictable.

In most hospital or university departments, rehearsals are routine practice, when time is checked and incomprehensible slides eliminated. Otherwise, the tape recorder is a valuable aid. For the speaker to hear his own talk may come as a shock, but it is better that he should hear it before his audience does. Time taken by rehearsal should be shorter than that allowed at the meeting. The best speakers are usually those who have given much time to practice and rehearsal. Some societies issue guidelines (Fig. 4.2) and these should be studied carefully.

An audience appreciates a firm Chairman. Methods of stopping a speaker vary. One way is by using lights, often a green warning light, followed by a red one. These are best placed on the speaker's desk out of sight of the audience. The speaker who continues in spite of a warning is rare, though at one international meeting a speaker had to be removed forcibly while he was still talking (Fig. 4.3).

Your paper has been selected because of its merit and interest. Some of the audience will know little about your subject. So please do everything possible to ensure that its message comes over clearly. Unless you happen to be an experienced lecturer, you may like to note that the best speakers would agree with the following:

1. Rehearsal.   This allows the time to be checked. If given 10 minutes, plan to do it in 8, for it often takes longer at the meeting. Incomprehensible slides are also eliminated at the rehearsal.

2. Speaking to the audience.   Reading from a typescript is often difficult to understand. It is better to speak from notes or to use slides as prompters.

3. Avoid too much detail.   Any technical subject presented to a mixed audience needs to be simplified. Sometimes tables, lists of figures and experimental methods can more appropriately be listed separately on a handout, available for those especially interested.

4. Clear slides.   Railway timetable slides which cannot be read unless the listener is equipped with field glasses are still shown. Slides must be designed simply, with lettering kept to 3 or 4 lines and graphs to 3 or 4 curves; tables should contain no more than four columns and four horizontal lines. Statistical data can often be better understood as histograms or diagrams. Lettering on a slide large enough to be read by the naked eye without projection ensures that everyone can read it; it also helps the speaker when sorting slides beforehand.

5. Electric torch.   Take care when using the electric torch as a pointer. Some speakers let it flicker aimlessly across the screen or room instead of keeping it on the lectern when not being used. But most slides, if carefully made, speak for themselves and need no pointer.

6. No need to read slides to the audience.   A common fault is to read the written slide word by word as if the listeners cannot read or are illiterate. It is often better to be silent while the audience reads, then perhaps draw attention to any particular points.

Fig. 4.2. Suggestions for speakers.

Causes of Obscurity

Sometimes the word "communication" is a misnomer and a euphemism. "Too many papers take the form of an inaudible soliloquy in front

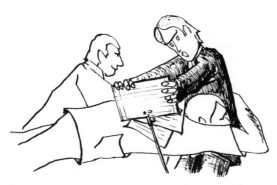

Fig. 4.3. . . . at one international meeting a speaker had to be removed forcibly while he was still talking.

of a series of invisible tables", according to a member of the pathological society (Williams 1965). A period of 2 minutes spent listening may cause complete confusion, whereas a brief conversation with the speaker enables the matter to be understood at once. One reason for this paradox is simple. In conversation, there is question and answer, a two-way channel of communication, but in speaking, the lecturer is neither questioned nor interrupted when he is not clear. Speakers confuse, and so quickly lose the interest of their audience for the following reasons:

Reading Instead of Speaking

Most societies have a rule that communications must be spoken and not read. Reading, unless by an expert, is impersonal; and a paper read rapidly in a monotone becomes almost meaningless. The natural rhythm of telling a story with its pauses and its contact with the audience is lost.

There are exceptions to this rule: international meetings when a speaker has to give a paper in another language, or those ritualistic occasions when a speaker is invited to deliver an address or oration which can be a dreary speech poorly read; the speaker may glue his eyes to his manuscript most of the time, occasionally lifting them to steal a glance at the audience as if to make sure that it is still there. However, it does not matter if a communication is read, provided that it has been written to be *heard* rather than *read*. When we speak, we repeat ourselves to make a point and therefore, if a paper is to be read, important points may have to be repeated. A paper should never be read in the same form as which it is to be published; it cannot be suitable for both media.

The main reason for someone reading his paper is that he is not confident at speaking, then a compromise is possible. The talk is first typed and practised again and again, the script gradually becoming unnecessary until only a few key phrases, suitably underlined, are needed. The result of this procedure is either a memorised speech helped by key phrases, or an extemporary speech prompted and held together by a manuscript.

Speaking Too Quickly

Speak slowly rather than fast, for speaking too quickly, as with a wind force of 10 to 12, confuses the audience; such a hurricane of words must be avoided and a suitable speed chosen. Also the pace can be varied, being slower for emphasis. Pauses are made between phrases and sentences rather than between individual words. Monotony is soporific and any variation of delivery helps. It is better to speak too loudly than too softly.

Too Much Detail

The material may consist of work carried out over one or more years. Any attempt to cram all the data into a short communication will obscure the message, as in an overcrowded amateur landscape painting with its lack of composition. A speech, like a painting, requires careful selection of material.

Inability to Explain

The wise can afford to be simple; many tend to cloak their ignorance in the long words of knowledge. Communications are commonly given as if the listener were perfectly familiar with the speaker's special interest, for someone working intensively for a long time on a piece of scientific research often cannot imagine what it is like not to know all that he knows. Perhaps the novice may also aim to impress rather than to inform or explain — to impress the most important or influential figures in the audience. It is, however, more likely that the influential, the "job-givers", will judge him more by his lucidity, not his profundity.

Jargon

As different branches of medicine develop, each creates its own vocabulary which is understood only by those routinely using it. This private language, or jargon, is necessary for easy communication and saves much time. However, many new words are introduced each year and there is no dictionary to explain them. This happens especially with an avant garde developing speciality; for example immunologists invented many new words and these sometimes differed in different centres even for the same things. One word, when unexplained, may cause a listener to stop and ponder; then contact with the speaker may never be regained. Similarly, abbreviations without explanation are frustrating to those unfamiliar with them; the standard ones such as ESR (erythrocyte sedimentation rate) or BP (blood pressure) are acceptable. But those that may be unfamiliar to anyone in the audience should always be explained, as they may be ambiguous (Fig. 4.4).

Soluble insulin
Serum iron
Saturation index
Sexual intercourse
Stimulation index
Système International d'Unités

Fig. 4.4. The many possible meanings of one abbreviation, SI.

Incomprehensible Slides

Just as the first requirement in a speaker is audibility, so the first requirement in a slide is legibility. Yet at nearly every meeting slides are shown which are unreadable unless the audience is equipped with field glasses; some even seem to resemble pages from a railway timetable.

Slides seem often to be a mere formality which confuse rather than illuminate. In the 10 or 15 seconds given to showing the slide, only three or four short lines can be read. Yet the slides may be packed with 10 or 20 lines of detail which the speaker has spent months in preparing. One slide projected at a meeting which the author attended contained 560 items (140 squares, each with four facts) — perhaps a record. There is only one thing worse than the dull overcrowded slide, and that is a series of such slides. The abuse of slides is common (Evans 1978) and the construction of clear slides is dealt with in Chap. 6.

Speakers are often obsessed with reading every word on the slide as if listeners are blind or illiterate; or worst of all, talk about something else while the audience is reading it. The audience must also have sufficient time to understand each slide — some are whisked away before the meaning of the abscissa and ordinate of a graph can be grasped. If there is reading matter, as in a last slide showing conclusions, the speaker should keep silent and allow the audience to read it then draw their attention to one or two points. A moment of silence also has a dramatic effect as in other art forms; for example, in the finale of the second symphony of Sibelius.

Delivery

The speaker must be seen and heard. The aim should be to interest rather than impress. To look at the audience is fundamental, though sometimes the lectern or even the slides are addressed, the back of the head alone being visible. Some look at their own slides too long and gaze in some perplexity, trying to recognise them — almost as if they had never seen them before; sometimes they may not have projected them beforehand for they may look different on the screen. The speaker should talk about the slide, not to it. Also, to be heard in spite of the poor acoustics of many lecture theatres and without help from an amplifying system, he must speak loud enough and in the right direction. This should not be to the front row, even though it is regrettably the custom of prominent people to congregate there; instead someone at the back of the hall should be addressed.

Lessons in elocution are occasionally needed. Some speakers frustratingly drop their voices at the end of sentences and others possess a groaning soporific voice as illustrated in the following account (Editorial 1962):

After the ritual draping of the microphone around his neck was completed, Dr. Winken B Nodd laid a sheaf of papers on the lectern. Then, crouching down as if to get as much cover as possible, he began. The entire address was delivered in a strained monotone which remained unaltered except for those periods, during and immediately after his illustrations, when he quickened his pace for a minute or two. He read on even when the tiny spot from his flashlight danced on the blurred and overloaded screen, and made intricate patterns on the wall and ceiling around him. Finally, when the chairman warned that his time was exhausted Nodd shuffled rapidly through the leaves of his manuscript to find his summary, read for another minute or two in stumbling haste, and departed. There were no questions.

Personality and Manner

Personality is important. One has only to think of a great teacher whose lectures stand out for their brilliance, clarity and wit, and are delivered with a showmanship which fixes them in the memory. By contrast, there is the other type of renowned figure who has talked on the same theme so many times before that the inspiration has gone, his manner has become tedious and his slides too well worn. The audience departs, pleased to have seen the celebrity, although disappointed with the lecture. A subordinate would have done the job of communication much better though he might have failed to attract an audience. The bright young man who paces up and down and treats his distinguished audience as if they were a class of students is an irritating bore. To speak to those who know little, yet to do so with humility, may not be easy.

The speaker should of course stand still. His dress is unimportant except that any bizarre aspect, such as a brightly coloured waistcoat, should be avoided as it attracts the attention of the audience unnecessarily. Some visual mannerisms are also very distracting. Repetitive movements such as putting spectacles on and taking them off or even a stance with hands in trouser pockets may disturb some.

It has been said that the research worker — the backroom boy who has no opportunity to teach — will naturally be unable to express his thoughts in public. Yet serious thinkers can usually convey their thoughts simply and analytically. Most bad communications are due to defects of technique which can be readily remedied. Perfection in speaking is mainly an acquired characteristic.

The Audience

A talk can hardly be considered a success without an audience. Yet, although the needs of consumers have been studied in other fields, little attention has been given to audiences; neither their wishes nor their suffering have been investigated to any extent. Interesting pilot studies have, however, been done. Medical student concentration during lectures has been studied by student feedback and results obtained can be used to improve lecturing performance (Stuart and Rutherford 1978). Another investigation focused on dreaming during scientific papers (Harvey et al. 1983); the audience was scanned surreptitiously with infrared viewers when the lights were dim and the prevalence of sleep recorded. Audits are needed to test the audience after a series of papers to find out how much has been understood. This would be precious little at some meetings.

Audiences may be classified as follows:

● All specialists in the same field as the speaker and likely to understand it all.

● All with a general background of medicine although only a few, perhaps 10% or less, are in the same specialty and likely to understand much of it.

● A lay audience such as those who watch television or listen to radio programmes.

The skill of the lecturer will be shown in addressing audiences in the last two categories, and his language (jargon) will have to be chosen carefully. In speaking to a lay audience, it will be impossible to be too precise, and intelligent listeners find this distasteful. Other speakers, however, overcome this successfully and succeed in making esoteric knowledge at least partly intelligible to the ordinary listener or reader.

The speaker must consider the type of audience as he prepares his talk, and details about his likely listeners may have to be sought. The same talk will have to be modified for different audiences. When in doubt, it is better to be too simple; for providing he is not patronising this will please everyone. The majority will depart pleased that it was so easily understood, and the ego of the few experts who knew it all will be duly elevated.

Technical Problems and How to Overcome Them

However careful the preparation, the possibilities of things going wrong on the occasion are considerable. Many are avoidable and checklists (Fig. 4.5) are helpful in trying to overcome every eventuality — though the unavoidable and unpredictable is a question of fate.

The Lectern

Technology, while improving efficiency, has made the modern lecture theatre more complex. Instead of an intimate setting with someone working a projector in the same room, the two actors, the lecturer and his projectionist, may be completely separated and unless there is a two-way microphone or telephone in the projectionist's booth, the only way to communicate is by signal and this must be agreed upon before the lecture. Furthermore, the modern trend is towards "do it yourself" and the projectionist may even disappear instead of acting as a stand-by in

```
┌─────────────────────────────────────────────────────────────┐
│                                                             │
│                   Check-list for lecturer                   │
│                                                             │
│  Before the lecture                                         │
│                                                             │
│         Time    ┌───┐    Date    ┌───┐    Place    ┌───┐    │
│                 └───┘            └───┘             └───┘    │
│         Subject ┌───┐         Duration of talk     ┌───┐    │
│                 └───┘                              └───┘    │
│              Audio-visual facilities                        │
│              (projector, overhead projector etc. available) ┌───┐
│                                                             └───┘
│         Type of audience  ┌───┐                             │
│                           └───┘                             │
│  Rehearsal                                                  │
│                                                             │
│         Timing correct    ┌───┐                             │
│                           └───┘                             │
│         Talk understood   ┌───┐                             │
│                           └───┘                             │
│         Slides legible    ┌───┐                             │
│                           └───┘                             │
│  On arrival (see lecture theatre and meet projectionist)    │
│                                                             │
│         Lectern light    ┌───┐   Control buttons   ┌───┐    │
│                          └───┘                     └───┘    │
│         Slides correctly ┌───┐   Who will operate slides ┌───┐
│         inserted in cassette └─┘                      └───┘ │
│                                                             │
│         Microphone       ┌───┐                             │
│                          └───┘                             │
│         Pointer          ┌───┐                             │
│                          └───┘                             │
│         Lighting (dimmed or blackout) ┌───┐                │
│                                       └───┘                │
│         Clock and its accuracy        ┌───┐                │
│                                       └───┘                │
└─────────────────────────────────────────────────────────────┘
```

Fig. 4.5. Check list for lecturer.

case the projector jams. Hence, it is most important to master technical aspects and to meet any projectionist beforehand.

Lecterns vary in size and shape. The ecclesiastical type typical of churches may be so big as to conceal small lecturers. In contrast, there is the unstable one which wobbles when gripped, so sapping the confidence of the speaker. Most difficult of all is the modern type where the control panel may be so complicated as almost to resemble that of a space ship, with 15 or more switches, often unlabelled. It is then best just to master the lights and projector switches. If anything else is touched, blinds may rise and fall, fans whirl — and possibly a trap door open as in lay theatres.

Discuss with the projectionist as to who is going to show the slides. The speaker may use a mobile hand switch (Fig. 4.6) and then it is important to know exactly what each knob is for, otherwise slides may dart about in different directions or be out of focus.

The lectern light should be checked, as it may have to be turned off when the radiographs or coloured slides are shown. It may be wise, if record cards are used for notes, to join these together by rings — just in case they are dropped and then put together in the wrong order.

Fig. 4.6. Hand switches for using the projector. The *arrows* on **a, c** and **d** indicate forward or backward movement of slides. Slide control on **b** is by the round button: a quick press moves the slide forwards while a longer press moves it backwards. The other buttons control focussing. The remote control switch without a cable (**d**) controls the projector with automatic focussing by an infra-red ray.

Microphones

A microphone, though indispensable in any large hall, may add to the difficulties of a speaker, for the apparatus itself can develop extraneous noises which compete for the listeners' attention. The fixed microphone needs care to avoid fluctuations in noise as the speaker's distance from it changes: even a mere turn of the head to look at a slide will lower the volume by several decibels. The mobile microphone, hung around the neck, is better. A chest microphone with a pocket radio transmitter is the most expensive but best arrangement. The worst is a portable microphone on a long flex. Anything can happen with this. It may be put down on the desk and accidentally covered by the notes; or an absent-minded speaker may inadvertently become coiled in the flex or even put the microphone in his pocket.

Lighting in the Auditorium

Complete darkness is undesirable and seldom necessary. The speaker has no eye contact with his listeners and it turns him into a disembodied voice, makes note-taking impossible and confuses latecomers trying to find seats. Most slides, apart from colour slides or radiographs, can be seen clearly if lights are just subdued. The worst infliction for an audience is to listen to a boring talk in the dark, sitting uncomfortably in a poorly ventilated theatre with no exit suitable for making a surreptitious escape.

Slides

However well a speaker has prepared his talk, it can be spoiled by trouble with slides, especially if they are put in upside down. Slides should be given to the projectionist in a box with the speaker's name marked on it and with instructions, preferably written, about lighting. Each should be numbered in case they are dropped and muddling occurs, and a spot put on the top of the inverted slide to ensure them being inserted the correct way. The best plan is to put in the slides oneself and there is usually a spare cassette available at meetings of several speakers; a card bearing the name of the speaker should be fixed to it.

The position of the rod or flashlight for pointing to the slide should be checked, as well as the position of chalk for the blackboard or pens for the overhead projector if this is to be used.

The Overhead Projector

An advantage is the fact that the speaker can face his audience rather than the blackboard, when his voice may become inaudible. It can also be used in normal lighting and can be written on during the lecture. However, it is preferable to prepare illustrations, charts and diagrams on the transparent sheets beforehand. Parts of a graph may be drawn on different sheets and these can be flipped over on hinges, for example the axes of a graph may be shown first and then the traces added one at a time; complex charts and diagrams may be filled up by this technique, especially when colours are used. X-rays and opaque objects may be projected onto the screen greatly magnified, using a transparent ruler if measurements are relevant.

Many presentations are spoiled because writing is too small, so always check that it can be read in the back row (Fig. 4.7). Also, the acetate sheets are often crammed with lettering, as in the railway timetable type of slide. Do not put more than ten lines on one sheet and make letters at least 5 mm high — and preferably larger. An easy way to ensure this is to place the transparent sheet on graph paper and to write between the lines (Fig. 4.8).

The infra-red transparency photocopier that photographs typescripts onto acetate sheets always produces lettering too small unless special large letters are fitted to the typewriter. A water-soluble pen like the Staedtler Lumocolor 315 allows the sheets to be used again and is available in a range of colours.

Films

The objection to showing a film is not only the risk of a technical fault, but also that much of it may be redundant. This is more likely if the

Use correct pens

Don't cram acetate sheets

Check for legibility (from back row)

Use correctly (face the audience)

Fig. 4.7. Instructions for using the overhead projector.

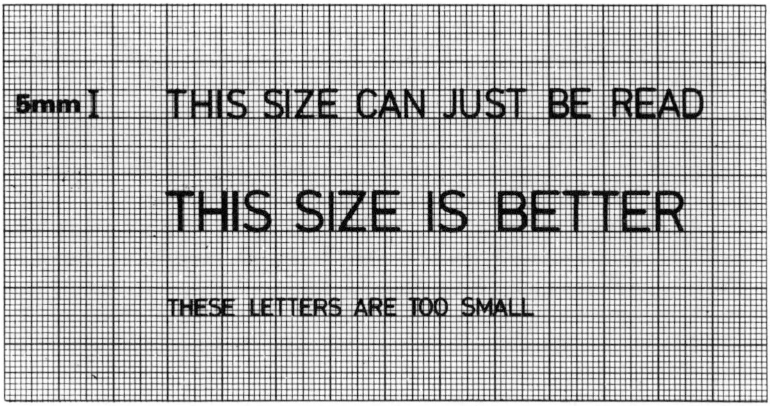

Fig. 4.8. Method of making sure that writing on the overhead projector is large enough.

speaker himself has made the film, for his amateurish efforts may blind him to its real values. A film must be edited ruthlessly. Less important detail may be speeded up while it is being projected. Furthermore, a film should be an essential part of a communication but sometimes the medical film at the end seems to appear almost as a reward for sitting through or perhaps even listening to the lecturer. Any form of illustration must be completely integrated into the talk and not used for its own sake.

Showing Objects

Objects, whether simple or complicated, should be concealed and revealed only at the moment when the speaker is talking about them, otherwise the attention of the audience may become fixed upon them. If small, objects can be kept in the cubby hole which is usually beneath the lectern and taken out when needed.

The Projectionist

The speaker, in any important meeting, depends upon the projectionist either to show his slides or to act as a stand-by if the speaker changes slides himself. The projectionist is apt to be taken for granted when all goes well but sometimes to be unfairly criticised when things go wrong. Some speakers forget that there is a limit to which slides can be shown, and that projectionists, being human, may make mistakes. If a slide is projected upside down, there are seven possible ways of showing it again wrongly; sometimes each is doggedly tried before the correct orientation is discovered. The way of inserting an unmarked slide is so simple that it should be taught to every student. It is first held in such a position that the writing it contains can be read; the slide is then rotated anti-clockwise through 180° before being placed in the cassette.

Incorrect focusing is the most frustrating fault, for fine slides can then be spoiled. The projectionist must have perfect sight or wear spectacles if necessary. Focusing upon lettering is easy but many slides depict patho-logical specimens or biochemical material which is a complete enigma to a lay person. The only person who can then focus properly is the speaker himself or someone who knows the subject. If there is no one to sit by and help him, a mark to focus upon should be inserted in the corner of difficult slides. One lecture by a distinguished visitor was ruined by bad focusing. Slide after slide was shown; brave efforts were made by the projectionist to focus upon strange forms and patterns but nobody offered to help and the audience sat in a frustrated and embarrassed silence.

The speaker himself may have an exaggerated idea of the definition of his slides if he has not seen them projected in a large hall. He then makes persistent and impossible demands for improving the focusing. The answer to this, according to one astute projectionist, is to put the slide completely out of focus and then to restore it to the same definition again, for the speaker is thereby placated.

Unless an automatic projector is used by the speaker, slides should always be shown by someone properly trained, a spare bulb should be readily available and there should be easy communication between projectionist and speaker, a matter that is less easy today than in the older and more intimate lecture theatres where speaker and projectionist were in the same room. The method of signalling about slides must be precise, as by using an electric or hand buzzer. It can be disconcerting when a projectionist who is perhaps listening to the talk and anxious to please, shows the next slide too soon.

Interpreters

Unobtrusive in their booths at international meetings, interpreters per-form a remarkable feat of communication — a marathon indeed as they listen without respite to speaker after speaker for several days. It is also remarkable that so few speakers heed them. Many read their speeches with a speed which bewilders any interpreter.

Interpreters usually prefer the speaker to speak in his own language rather than attempt another which, in any event, will have to be translated. Speaking into the microphone is essential, else the interpreter may lose contact. It is also confusing if he suddenly changes to another language, perhaps as a courtesy to the hosts or to display linguistic prowess. Some even speak in one language while their slides are written in another; this is also confusing and should be avoided except perhaps for captions on graphs or diagrams. A copy of the communication should reach the interpreter usually 10 days before the meeting.

Speaking slowly is also a courtesy to listeners whose native tongue is not one of the official languages of the meeting. If, alas, a speaker must read his communication, the speed limit should not exceed 120 words a minute (approximately one and a half minutes for each double-spaced typewritten page); and pauses are essential after each definite point, to allow the audience to think about it.

Symposia, Colloquia and Panel Discussions

Symposia, colloquia and panel discussions all require several speakers, and thus provide the stimulating effect of different personalities with different views. Discipline and careful planning are essential, for these conferences can be wrecked by one speaker talking for too long.

A symposium referred originally to a drinking party after a banquet; now it implies a meeting where several speakers deliver short addresses on one or more related topics. A colloquium refers to a conference or seminar in which several lecturers take leading parts. It is ironic that the word colloquial means familiar conversation, for the greatest obstacle in colloquia today is the incomprehensibility of the speakers. Each talks in the technical jargon of his own specialty and there is no dictionary for this, so in some meetings few participants understand each other. Such meetings, although intended to encourage cross-fertilisation of ideas, may fail owing to the difficulty of communication. This can be overcome in various ways:

● By issuing a glossary of terms to all members of the audience.

● By writing terms and their meanings on a blackboard during each communication.

● By allowing the Chairman to interrupt and ask for an explanation whenever he thinks it necessary.

A panel discussion, to be successful, requires a good Chairman, speakers who can speak succinctly and with humour, and careful planning. In a preliminary meeting, speakers should get to know each other and consider the best way to run the discussion; problems and suitable questions are considered and listed. If the audience is going to participate, one listener can be briefed with a question to start the discussion going. Strict control of timing is important and any introductions must be brief. Spontaneity is spoiled by lengthy answers and by showing slides. Spice is supplied by conflict between the speakers.

The Case Demonstration

Case demonstrations form the basis of many medical meetings. Often, to impress his fellows with the thoroughness with which he has "worked up" his case, the tyro gives too much detail and bores them. Careful thought and editing are essential; no one wants to hear about a man's bunions or varicose veins unless they are relevant. Surgeons are apt to spend too much time describing unnecessary technical details of an operation when addressing a general audience of doctors. The story of the patient's symptoms should be told in the order of their occurrence and an account given of the various problems and pitfalls which were encountered before the diagnosis was finally made. This provides interest and suspense, factors so often missing in the conventional account in a journal; for the customary plan of an article — introduction, investigations and discussion — is an artificial pattern which explains why articles may be dull.

It is advisable to rehearse with the patient, for the speaker can easily be deflated. "This is a man of 45 years", begins the speaker "No", interrupts the patient, "I am 43", and so on. A tête-à-tête between speaker and patient can develop and must be avoided. Abnormal physical signs may mysteriously disappear when one attempts to demonstrate them during a meeting, even though they have been checked carefully just before.

Lectures

Lectures have been derided for centuries. Artists such as Hogarth have satirised them in pictures, showing the boredom of inattentive listeners. Critics have described them as a relic of times before the printing press was invented. Doctor Samuel Johnson said: "Lectures were once useful; but now, when all can read, and books are so numerous, lectures are unnecessary. If your attention fails and you miss a part of the lecture, it is lost; you cannot go back as you do upon a Book." (Quoted by James Boswell in his *Life of Samuel Johnson*, April 15, 1781.)

There are varied reasons for such criticism today. One is that universities seldom take any steps to train their lecturers, in contrast to other institutions such as the Church or the teaching profession. This is surprising, because a lecture, especially to a large audience, is analogous to a stage performance. No one would expect to succeed on the professional stage without training. Nor would anyone expect to give a radio talk without rehearsal and valuable assistance from a producer. Doctors and scientists, however, lecture by the light of nature and without guidance.

The Special Role of Lectures

Seeing the lecturer is an important reason for attending a lecture. The man of distinction, or the expert in a particular field of research, previously merely a name of reference, comes alive and real, although not always to his advantage! He will present the subject in perspective, giving alternative views and stimulating the interest, thought and speculation of the listeners, and will probably say much that cannot be obtained from books or journals. Furthermore, an expectant curiosity and excitement attends any live performance and is important in encouraging receptivity.

The Problems of the Lecturer

Lecturing successfully is a most difficult form of speech, for the interest of a passive and sometimes uninterested audience has to be retained for 40–50 minutes. This, in the world of drama, would be considered almost impossible for the experienced actor, as Karl Darrow emphasised in his essay *How to Address the American Physical Society*[2]:

> The actor has all the advantages. He is speaking lines written for him by a master of the art of commanding the interest of an audience . . . He has a gift for acting, and also a long experience in the art; otherwise he would not be in the cast. Even so, he is not allowed to speak his lines in any way that occurs to him. Every phrase, every inflexion, every gesture, even the position that he is to take on the stage, has been tested or even prescribed by a professional director, who does not hesitate to give him mandatory instructions or even to alter the lines if they seem ineffective.
>
> One might assume that assured of such splendid collaboration, the dramatist would write a play two hours long without a break, and the manager would be content to offer the play in a barn with benches for the seats. This is apparently not the view of those who are experienced in such matters. Ample intermissions are provided, and an act which runs for so long as an hour is sufficiently rare to cause the critics to mention it. Usually the theatre has comfortable chairs and is well

ventilated or even air conditioned. All this is provided to induce people to come to a play for the apprehension of which, with rare exceptions, no intellectual effort is demanded.

Now consider the physicist. He has thought out his own lines, and is not always proficient in this not altogether easy art. He has little or no training in the art of elocution, and no director has rehearsed him. His subject requires a considerable amount of mental effort on the part of his listeners. His listeners themselves are usually uncomfortable and sometimes acutely so. This may be because the chairs are uncomfortable, or because the room is hot and stuffy, or because the programme has already been running for an hour or more without break; or two or all three of these conditions may exist together. Laurence Olivier or Helen Hayes might well quail at the prospect of having to sway an audience under such conditions.

Some are born good lecturers; needing no instruction, their success may be due to their enthusiasm, originality, sincerity, feeling for showmanship, as well as personal qualities which enable them to attract and sway audiences. Others are ineffective and will always remain so — "shifting dullness' was the nickname given to one. The latter may be unable to explain subjects simply, or have a defect such as a soft voice which only reaches the second row of the audience.

Most lecturers learn by experience or by watching others lecture, and some may ask a friend or colleague to listen and criticise. Some may possess faults which, if corrected, would make all the difference to their success. Looking at the audience is elemental although some look out of the window, at the ceiling or at their typescript. Others, perhaps from the monotony of lecturing or from familiarity with the audience, develop curious habits. Walking up and down like a caged animal is not uncommon, and the audience may become preoccupied with the distance travelled instead of the lecture itself.

The Object of the Lecture

The aim should be to rouse enthusiasm and to stimulate thought. "For the mind does not require filling like a bottle . . . it only requires kindling to create in it an impulse to think independently and an ardent desire for the truth" might well have been stated in a modern symposium on education, although it was written in the first century AD by Plutarch in his essay *On Listening to Lectures*. Mr Winston Churchill, during a speech at Bristol University in 1929, stated "The most important thing about education is appetite".

All that can be hoped for in most lectures is to drive home a selected number of points, well defined, properly emphasised and arranged in appropriate order. It is a mistake to attempt to give a running commentary on the whole subject or to cover the whole ground; this is better left to books or distributed in handouts.

How to Sustain Interest

If the level of interest could be measured during a lecture, various curves might be obtained. When listening to a pioneer telling of his discovery, interest would start at a high level and probably continue so until the end. When an interesting subject was delivered by a dull lecturer, the high initial interest would fall rapidly. The curve for an average lecture would probably rise in the first few minutes and gradually fall as time went on. Hence, the lecturer should plan his talk with this in mind. Methods of sustaining interest are as follows:

● *Rhetoric.* Skill in speaking is the way orators hold and sway audiences. Though this ability is often inborn, anyone can improve his diction by apt choice of words, and by avoiding worn-out words and clichés which have ceased to convey anything to the hearer.

● *Quoting examples.* Describing a concrete example aids understanding and is a welcome change from the abstract substance of so many lectures. The study of medicine provides many opportunities for this: the story of an interesting case will hold the attention of almost any audience if it is relevant and well told.

● *Humour.* Humour revives interest and gives light relief. Medicine is often difficult but there is no reason why it should at the same time be dull. Yet it is an art to be able to use humour successfully; taste and discretion are essential, the temptation to overdo it being resisted. Too many jokes, especially if irrelevant, may cause annoyance and the audience then begins to laugh *at* and not *with* the lecturer. Slides can give opportunities for humorous relief and may be used to reinforce serious ideas.

● *Setting problems.* A problem is presented to listeners so that they can take part in thinking of various solutions.

● *Provocation.* The audience may be provoked into thinking by various ways. One is to attack accepted hypotheses and traditional ideas.

● *Mentioning contemporary problems.* Some subjects may already have been surrounded by an aura of interest, having been headlines in the daily press. Advantage can be taken of this.

● *Allowing interruptions.* Encouraging listeners to take part by asking questions during a lecture is only successful when the audience is small. The questioner may irritate the rest of the audience who, feeling frustrated because they do not share his difficulty, consider that the progress of the lecture is being delayed.

● *Visual aids.* Visual aids are used to introduce greater variety in a lecture than is possible in books and are important in reinforcing ideas, as memory is so often visual. Slides are dealt with elsewhere (Chap. 6). Drawing during a lecture provides the excitement of a live performance and the interest of seeing a picture in the making. There may also be the malicious relish of watching closely to see if the lecturer goes wrong; suspense can be heightened by the pregnant pause as if thinking of the next move or by spelling an occasional word wrongly. Some lecturers provide prepared diagrams and pictures on the overhead projector to be completed during the lecture. The reason why lectures and talks on television often are so much better than conventional ones is that, apart from being better prepared, use is made of a greater variety of audio-visual aids.

Handouts

It is best to distribute handouts at the end of the talk, otherwise attention may be lost while they are being read. Although some lecturers spurn handouts as encouraging spoon feeding, most listeners welcome them, for they avoid the burden of regular note-taking. Even for those skilled at shorthand, the difficulty of doing two things at the same time — understanding the lecture and noting it on paper — may be insurmountable. The contents of handouts may consist of one or more of the following:

1. A summary of the lecture
2. An outline of the structure of the lecture — the main and subsidiary idea and elaborations
3. An accurate record of some of the details
4. A record of complex data
5. Ideas to stimulate thinking
6. Useful references

Handouts containing essential facts — a summary of the lecture — are helpful for the lecturer, especially if he is absent minded. He can then relax and enjoy lecturing without having to worry whether he has missed saying something that he intended to say. Those listed under 3, 5 and 6 can also be used by speakers giving communications at meetings or taking part in symposia.

Pity the Speaker

The speaker needs sympathy and care for his welfare whether he is a novice giving a communication motivated by the "publish or perish" incentive — so necessary for obtaining jobs — or an established speaker. He may be apprehensive and have travelled a long distance, so a warm welcome and sustenance are needed.

The academician and humourist Stephen Leacock (1958) described the hazards of speaking in an essay *We Have With Us Tonight (How it Feels to be a Lecturer)*, and Stephen Lock (1978), editor of the British Medical Journal, whilst stating that he usually had a good time when invited to speak, described misadventures that we all experience in *Nice People With No Manners*; the following, adapted from his article, are suggestions for those organising meetings.

1. Tell the speaker his precise subject, audience and length of time.

2. Do turn up if you invited the speaker or at least let him know beforehand that he will be met by a substitute.

3. Arrange a parking space and see that a porter at the gate knows that he is coming.

4. Start the meeting on time.

5. Find out about your speaker's career. Few things are more embarrassing than having audibly to prompt a chairman about his name, past and what he is doing now. (Leacock described occasions when he was introduced as the wrong person.)

6. Write the speaker a letter of thanks — and sign it. Sometimes no bread-and-butter letter follows or the thank-yous may even be duplicated and unsigned.

7. Pay your speaker his expenses and try to estimate what these are. Avoid giving him a complicated form to fill in.

8. Give your speaker something, though preferably not a cheque. His secretary could be asked what he would like — this may be a book or gift token or wine. Such a symbolic gesture is no more expensive than most honoraria and may be cheaper, apart from being more acceptable.

9. Finally, if you are going to publish the proceedings of a meeting, give your contributors notice. When a speaker has lectured from notes and slides there are few more depressing pieces of news than to be told at the end of the session that that Association's standing orders require you to produce a written text.

References

Darrow KK (1961) How to address the American Physical Society. Physics Today 14:20–23

Editorial (1962) The onus on communicants. Can Med Assoc J 86:332

Editorial (1964) The art of omission. JAMA 188:313

Evans M (1978) The abuse of slides. Br Med J 1:905–908

Gowers E Sir (1973) The complete plain words. Revised by Sir Bruce Fraser. Her Majesty's Stationery Office, London

Harvey RF, Schullinger MB, Stassinopoulos A, Winkle E (1983) Dreaming during scientific papers: effects of added extrinsic material. Br Med J 2:1916–1919

Leacock S (1958) We have with us tonight (how it feels to be a lecturer). In: Priestley JB (ed) The Bodley Head Leacock. The Bodley Head, London, pp 174–187

Lock S (1978) Nice people with no manners. Br Med J 2:1774–1775

Stuart J, Rutherford RJD (1978) Medical student concentration during lectures. Lancet II:514–516

Williams PC (1965) Suggestions for speakers and standards for slides. Insti Biol J 12:65–70

5. What the Critical Reader Looks for in an Original Article: A Guide for Writers

William F. Whimster

> *The craftsman is proud and careful of his tools;*
> *the surgeon does not operate with an old razor*
> *blade, the sportsman fusses happily and long over*
> *the choice of rod, gun, club or racquet. But the*
> *man that is working in words, unless he is a*
> *professional writer (and not always then), is*
> *singularly neglectful of his instruments.*
>
> Ivor Brown
> (Quoted in the Complete Plain Words by
> Sir Ernest Gowers. Pelican, 1963, p.69)

Our aim is to help the writer to look at the draft of his article through the eyes of the reader to see if he has done what the reader needs. We are not saying: "You should do this or that". We are saying: "Write. Then use the criteria in this chapter to look critically at what you have written, and to identify changes which would make the article easier for the reader to take in." Therefore this chapter concentrates on item 12 in Fig. 5.1.

Most readers have to read many original articles to keep up to date. So they like a recognisable format in which the individual components are easy to find and read separately. Fortunately, the IMRAD structure (Introduction, Methods, Results and Discussion) has evolved. Most readers now understand this format and a writer should use it unless he can convince the editor that the readers will appreciate his message more easily in another format. This is seldom the case in presenting the results of research.

Readers also like original articles in which the message is clearly defined and not surrounded by distractions. A distraction is anything in the writing that unintentionally raises a question in the reader's mind (see the examples in a later section). The reader then looks for the answer instead of continuing along the train of thought planned for him by the author. There are many types of distraction, all of which slow down and irritate the reader, although he often does not realise exactly what the distraction is.

1. What is the message?
2. Why is the paper worth writing?
3. Who will read the paper?
4. Who will the authors be?
5. Which journal?
   Read its instructions to authors.
   Note how the references are quoted in the text.
   Is the reference list Harvard or numerical (sequential or alphabetical)?
   Does it accept Vancouver style?
   How many copies are required?
6. Write the first drafts
   of the introduction — why did we start?
   of the methods — what did we do?
   of the results — what did we find?
   of the discussion — what do the results mean?
   in whatever order suits you,
   with references in Harvard style at this stage.
   Make file cards and file them sequentially.
7. Draft tables.
8. Draft figures and figure legends.
9. Check the article to ensure that the material is in the right sections and that the meaning is clear. Amend where necessary.
10. Draft the remaining parts — abstract, running title, key words, acknowledgements.
11. Give it to a critical colleague to read according to the precepts outlined in this chapter.
12. Discuss the critical colleague's suggestions with him.
13. Amend the paper in the light of the suggestions.
14. Check the references against the originals.
15. Check all numerical material — in the text, tables and figures.
16. Write a covering letter to introduce the article to the editor.
17. Send it off to the journal.

Fig. 5.1. Check-list for writing an original paper.

Problems of Foreign Writers

Authors whose first language is not English can be reassured that English authors have just as much trouble with distractions. Ten years of giving "medical writing" courses in many parts of the world and of supervising the English of the articles in *Annals of Clinical Research* (one of three journals published in English by the Finnish Medical Society Duodecim) have shown me that, if the author has good work to present, "being foreign" adds only a little to the problems of producing an original article acceptable to editors and readers.

The Value of a Critical Colleague

Although a few medical and scientific authors write original articles in memorable prose, most authors, even the most senior and experienced, do not (Fig. 5.2). So a colleague who understands the principles of this chapter and who is prepared to act as an independent reader is a great asset. This "colleague" treatment is not particularly concerned with the scientific content of the article — constructive criticism of the scientific content should come from someone else, such as one's supervisor or departmental head. Incidentally, it is often very difficult for a hierarchical head (professor or director) to subject himself to the "colleague"

Fig. 5.2. Writer's block. One remedy is to sit down for a fixed time, perhaps 15 minutes, and write non-stop about any aspect of the subject which you prefer.

treatment, or to find a suitable colleague to do it with him. Nevertheless his articles are vastly more readable and his messages conveyed more effectively if he does so.

The "colleague" treatment works best if the author gives the colleague a copy of the article to write his suggestions on and then discusses them face to face. The author's verbal answers to "Why do you say that?" or "Is that logical?" are often much clearer than what he has written, and can sometimes be incorporated almost verbatim.

The best arrangement is a dual one in which each partner acts as the "critical colleague" for the other. Nevertheless many authors find it impractical to develop a satisfactory relationship at all. Such an author has, therefore, to be his own "critical reader" and must learn to look at his own writing objectively to identify and remove the distractions himself.

The Structure of the Article

Title

The title is what catches the reader's eye and deserves careful thought. It should be short yet sufficiently descriptive. Abbreviations should not be used. Paradoxical, obscure or misleading titles help neither reader nor cataloguer. The title also provides information used by computerised information storage systems. Most of the existing bibliographic compilation programs are of the multiple entry type, so that a paper is classified under several headings. For example, if a paper is entitled "The effects of exercise on free fatty acids in the blood", it would probably be classified under "fatty acids", "metabolism of fatty acids", "exercise" and "blood"; but if it is entitled "the effects of exercise on the composition of free fatty acids in the blood: a study in rats using chromatographic techniques", it would also be classified under "composition of fatty acids", "chromatography of fatty acids" and "fatty acids in rats" and thus reach a wider audience.

If the title does not indicate that the contents come within the reader's range of interests when they do, the reader may miss a useful paper. If the title suggests that the contents do come within his range of interests but they do not, the reader will be irritated. So information must be packed carefully but accurately into the title. A title must therefore be judged by the items of information it contains and whether they are accurate.

Take "Bronchial plasmacytoma identified by immunoperoxidase technique on paraffin embedded section" (Okada et al. 1982). This title could be analysed as follows:

The article is about a plasmacytoma, which occurred in the bronchus (a rare site), and it really was a plasmacytoma because the "immunoperoxidase technique on paraffin embedded section" ruled out other possibilities. In fact "on paraffin embedded section" could be deleted because readers of this journal can be expected to know that the immunoperoxidase technique is usually applied to paraffin embedded sections. In addition it can be inferred that the article is more about the tumour than its identification or the title would have read "Identification of a bronchial plasmacytoma by the immunoperoxidase technique". The title might therefore be revised to "Bronchial plasmacytoma identified by the immunoperoxidase technique".

This still gives the reader no idea why the case was thought to be worth publishing. In the article, however, one finds that it was a unique case of bronchial plasmacytoma with local amyloid deposition. Is this of more interest than how it was identified? Would a subheading help? "Bronchial plasmacytoma with amyloid deposition: report of a unique case and review of the literature" might be acceptable, provided the "literature" (a term for "published work", to which some readers object because they prefer to retain the term for the works of writers of a higher literary class, such as Shakespeare) is competently reviewed. That would be a matter for further discussion between the author and his colleague.

We believe that it is well worth analysing the title in this way to make sure that it contains the elements of the paper that it is intended to convey.

The Bradford Hill Questions

As already mentioned, there are considerable advantages to readers in the IMRAD (Introduction, Methods, Results and Discussion) structure, provided each section is used properly. In 1965 Bradford Hill put forward the following questions with which to test the individual components of this:

Introduction .... Why did they start?
Methods .... What did they do?
Results .... What did they find?
Discussion .... What do the results mean?

The "Bradford Hill questions" make a powerful analytical tool not only for authors but also for many types of reader, including, for example, those preparing articles for "journal clubs".

The Introduction

Here the question is "Why did they start?". The introduction, indeed the entire paper, must be intelligible to the readers of the journal chosen, however specialised the subject, but it need not be long and pompous. An effective, simple, and adaptable format is as follows:

> Smith reported that the earth was flat (Smith 1965*), but Jones has presented evidence that the earth is round (Jones 1974*). We devised a new technique to determine whether either of these assertions was correct. We present the results in this paper.

This introduces the reader to the state of knowledge before the research was started, defines the gap in knowledge which the research will fill, and states what the authors set out to do. It does not review the history of the subject from the time of Pythagoras to the present day. It does not identify all the other gaps in knowledge. It does not include methods, results or discussion.

It is surprising how often the question "Why did they start?" cannot be answered after reading the introduction.

Methods

The question here is "What did they do?" The answer must include what patients, animals or specimens the results were obtained from, what techniques were used to obtain them and what statistical techniques were used to analyse the results. Many readers read the methods section first to see if they can understand what the authors did, and whether there is enough information for them to repeat the work themselves. If there is not they cannot judge whether the results are of any value and there is no point in reading any more.

This section should also give the reasons for selecting the experimental design of the project. It may be worth dividing the section into subsections, with particular attention to the way in which people or animals were selected or handled.

---

*Asterisk indicates fictitious reference, here and elsewhere.

Patients, Animals, Specimens

Patients and animals are living things; they are not inanimate "material". This section should be called "Material and Methods" only if inanimate specimens have been used.

One must check the numbers of patients, how they are grouped, the criteria for inclusion and exclusion, whether informed consent was obtained, and indeed whether the experiment or trial had been approved by an ethical committee and conformed to the ethical standards of the Declaration of Helsinki (World Medical Association 1964). Similar checks will be made if animals were used. Failure to fulfil the ethical requirements will almost certainly mean that the journal will reject the article.

Techniques

Many authors are confused about how much detail to include. One has to guess how familiar with one's methods readers of the journal concerned are likely to be and give enough detail for them to assess the validity of the results and, if necessary, to repeat the work themselves. Techniques for which there are already clear published descriptions (many such descriptions are not clear) in an accessible form (journals are generally more accessible than books) do not have to be described again, but modifications to published techniques must be very carefully described so that the reader can marry the original description with the present description.

If drug trials or similar experiments are being described, the reader needs a clear description of the design of the trial, including how the number of individuals needed to produce a valid result was arrived at, exactly what was done to each group, as well as what individuals dropped out and why, together with details of randomisation and whether a single or double blind technique was used.

Statistics

It is no longer acceptable to the reader for the results simply to be manipulated statistically in the results section without explanation. The reader needs a clear account of what statistical techniques have been used. The authors should also bear in mind that editors often now obtain a statistical opinion before accepting an article. They are also increasingly of the view that it is unethical to publish results based on inadequate statistical analysis because clinical practices based on such results may harm patients (Altman 1980).

Statistical matters are discussed in more detail in Chap. 7.

Results

The description of results obtained throughout the development of a research project is the heart of the publication. It is the communication of facts, measurements and observations gathered by the research worker. Inexperienced research workers usually describe their results in chronological order. But it is usual to repeat experiments, with slight variations in one or more variables, and for the experimental design to be simplified as the variables that control a phenomenon are identified. It is often more appropriate, therefore, to start with results that are easiest to interpret, regardless of when they were obtained.

The results section must answer the question "What did they find?" Ideally the results should be set out in tables so that all the raw data are available for the reader to analyse for himself. The editor seldom has enough space for this, so tables or figures showing processed data are acceptable; the authors should, however, state that the raw data are available from them on request. The results that support or do not support what the authors set out to show (see "Introduction") are the important ones and the reader is helped if these are expressed clearly in this section.

Discussion

It is in the discussion that the author incorporates his contribution into existing knowledge. When discussing the conclusions of other research workers, one should clearly state their origin and quote them correctly, bearing in mind that unfavourable comparisons with previous work do not increase the merit of one's own work. This is not to say that mistakes in reasoning or experimental design should not be criticised, but it is better to show how one's own results correct a false impression or lend themselves to a different interpretation. In medicine and biology phenomena are so complex that it is rare for there to be just one interpretation.

Inexperienced research workers often find it difficult to attain an adequate level of assurance in their conclusions, and write, for example, "This seems to suggest . . . " Such lack of assurance should be avoided.

The discussion should answer the question "What do the results mean?" and possibly "What gaps in knowledge remain to be filled?"

The reader is helped if the main results are summarised at the beginning of the discussion, and also if the aspects of the subject thought worthy of discussion are clearly identified, if necessary with subheadings.

Some authors think that they will be criticised if they do not mention every previous publication in the field but it is necessary only to identify previous results or comments which illuminate or which are illuminated by the present results. The reader is greatly helped by a final paragraph in which the message of the article is firmly stated. It is helpful to point out where further gaps in knowledge could usefully be filled but the blanket statement "Further research is needed", although usually true, will suggest to the critical reader that the author has not thought it out. When the paper throws light on new aspects of the subject, it is useful if the author says whether he intends to explore them. This need not be very detailed but must be an accurate and honest guide to fellow research workers who may be planning experiments in the same areas.

Acknowledgements

This section of the paper should consist simply of "We wish to thank . . . " all those who deserve recognition for their contributions but who have not made a significant intellectual contribution and are therefore not included as authors. Gratitude may, for example, be given to a physician who has allowed his patients to be studied or to a sponsoring organisation for drugs or equipment.

Editors may require authors to obtain written permission from each person acknowledged by name because readers will assume that anyone acknowledged endorses the data and the conclusions.

References

The term "references" is generally used in preference to "bibliography", which, strictly speaking, means a complete list of everything that has been published on a subject, but, in practice, is often used rather imprecisely to mean "further reading".

References are provided to indicate the sources from which the author has obtained information, but the value of an article is not measured by the number of references and they should not be included merely to show erudition.

Garfield (1982) has clearly expressed our attitude to references: "The importance of citing sources in scientific publications should not be taken lightly. After all, citations are the reward system of scientific publication. To cite someone is to acknowledge that person's impact on subsequent work. Citations are the currency by which we repay the intellectual debt we owe our predecessors. Furthermore, failing to cite sources deprives other researchers of the information contained in those sources and may lead to duplication of effort". On the other hand the sources quoted must be relevant and they must be quoted accurately.

Many authors are confused about how to quote references in the text and how to construct the list of references. This is best done in three stages:

1. Start off by writing in the names of the authors and date of each reference as it arises. Thus:

Jones and Bloggs (1962*) reported hypercalcaemia in three cases of sarcoidosis, although hypocalcaemia has also been reported (Asquith and Tate 1965*; Meredith et al. 1971*).

At the same time write the full details for each reference (all authors and their initials; full title; full journal or book reference with inclusive page numbers) on a file card and file the cards in order of appearance in the text.

2. When the paper is complete check the "instructions to authors" of the journal. The "Harvard system", as above, may be what is required. Otherwise the journal may use numbers in the text to mark the references in one of two ways: in the order in which they arise:

*Jones and Bloggs[1] reported hypercalcaemia in three cases of this condition, although hypocalcaemia has also been reported[2,3].

Or they may be taken from the reference list after it has been arranged alphabetically. In that case the file cards must be rearranged in alphabetical order by the surnames of the first authors and numbered. Those numbers must then be inserted in the text to give:

Jones and Bloggs[2] reported hypercalcaemia in three cases of this condition, although hypocalcaemia has also been reported[1,3].

3. The list of references is then typed out either alphabetically (Harvard system), or numerically in the order in the text, or numerically in alphabetical order.

If the journal has agreed to the Vancouver style (International Committee of Medical Journal Editors 1982) the references should be typed out in that style and the editor will be responsible for putting them into the format he requires. It is unfortunate that the Vancouver style includes abbreviated forms of journal titles — it would be more convenient for authors, who may not have the *Index Medicus* abbreviations readily to hand, if full titles were required. For other journals the "instructions to authors" must be consulted.

The reader works on the understanding that every reference quoted has been seen by the authors and that it does say what it is quoted as saying. With interlibrary loan systems and photocopying services, it is now possible, although expensive, to see every reference. It is just permissible, however, to quote an unobtainable reference as "Smith (1832*), cited by Adams (1973*)". Adams is then responsible for what he says Smith said.

We have found from bitter experience that it is essential to check every detail of every reference with the original, not just with the reference card, before sending the paper off — many mistakes are always found, although it is unusual for them to be so extensive that the reference is totally untraceable. Flawed references can greatly distract the reader.

Abstract

Although the abstract appears first in the article, it is best written last because it must contain the essence of the introduction (the purpose of the study), the methods, the main findings (with specific results and their statistical significance) and main conclusions. The style can be impersonal and condensed. It is not an introduction to the article and is not intended to be read as part of the article. It should not contain material that is not in the article.

There is much confusion about the nature and function of abstracts, summaries and synopses. A summary was once the summing up of the message at the end of an article. Then editors put it first so readers could see if they wished to read the whole article. Then it began to be used by abstracting journals so more care had to be given to its contents. It is now best called an abstract although some journals still call it a summary. A synopsis, on the other hand, is a brief note of the contents of the article, usually prepared by the journal editor rather than the author. Synopses are seldom used.

In the Vancouver style the abstract is limited to 150 words and indeed some computers are programmed to accept only 150 words — subsequent words are just omitted.

Key words are usually typed below the abstract. These are three to ten words or short phrases intended to assist indexers in crossindexing the article. Terms from the medical subject headings list from *Index Medicus* should be used when possible.

Examination of the Text

The critical colleague examines each paragraph, sentence and word in the text to locate ambiguities and distractions whose elimination will get the message into the journal reader's brain more easily. Many of these distractions are examples of simple misusages of the eight parts of speech (noun, pronoun, adjective; verb, adverb; preposition, conjunction; and article) or of their positions in sentences. Some common examples of easily corrected misunderstandings that may be looked for are given below. Readers may like to supplement these examples with the entertaining and instructive ones in *The Complete Plain Words* (Gowers 1962), and *Fowler's Modern English Usage* (Gowers 1968).

Why Use Paragraphs?

"The purpose of paragraphing is to give the reader a rest", wrote Sir Ernest Gowers (1968, p.434). It is the unit of thought or information, and thus should encompass just one idea, and then give the reader a mental and visual break. Many authors like to start by pouring out their ideas with minimal paragraphing, especially when writing the discussion. Some writing unfortunately never gets any more attention, but, for the reader's sake, the next stage must be to analyse the arrangement of the ideas and to check their juxtapositions and to order them into paragraphs. If it is a long discussion it is a good idea also to put in subheadings so that the reader can obtain an overview of the text before reading it in detail.

Sentence Checking

Each sentence is checked to ensure that it has a subject and a verb, and that they agree. For example, many readers will waste a few seconds working out what is wrong with: "The new group of drugs were associated with many adverse reactions". In fact the subject is "group" which is singular, and the verb is "were" which is plural — it should be corrected to "was".

Distracting Clauses and Phrases

When the main subject and verb of a sentence have been identified, the subordinate clauses and phrases can be checked. Adjectival clauses and phrases must refer to specific nouns, and adverbial clauses and phrases must refer to specific verbs. The difficulties an author can get into are shown by:

The results could not be analysed because the serum creatinine had not been recorded except in one case which was unfortunate.

The adjectival clause "which was unfortunate" refers to "case" and does not make sense. It is distracting to have to work out that the author meant: "It was unfortunate that the results could not be analysed because the serum creatinine had not been recorded except in one case".

Further difficulties arise with commenting and defining adjectival clauses and phrases:

1. "The dogs, whose spleens had been removed, all died" means that all the dogs died and, as a comment, that the dogs had had their spleens removed.

2. "The dogs whose spleens had been removed all died" defines the group of dogs, and implies that there were other groups of dogs.

3. It is impossible to determine the meanings of the sentences: "The dogs, whose spleens had been removed all died" or "The dogs whose spleens had been removed, all died", without asking the author.

An adverbial clause or phrase refers to a verb and should be placed next to that verb. In: "The bronchoscopy was performed by the same member of the team under general anaesthesia", was it the member who was under general anaesthesia? If "under general anaesthesia" refers to "performed" it is adverbial, not adjectival, and must be moved next to "performed" to make that clear: "The bronchoscopy was performed under general anaesthesia by the same member of the team". This is more likely to be what the author meant.

It is often better to simplify sentences by splitting the subordinate clauses and phrases off and making them into sentences of their own.

Carelessness with Nouns and Adjectives

Whether nouns are plural or singular may also distract the reader. For example, "28 patients had a prepyloric ulcer on gastroscopy" probably means that they each had one, so perhaps it should be "28 patients had prepyloric ulcers on gastroscopy". But that reads as though individual patients could have had more than one prepyloric ulcer. The author must rewrite it to express clearly what he does mean.

Noun clusters, in which nouns are used as adjectives, such as "the patient liver enzyme status", should be looked at critically. What is a "patient liver"? or "patient status"?

Adjectival clusters, such as "clear cellular atypia", should also be looked at critically. Does the author mean an atypia of clear cells or that cellular atypia was obvious?

Pronouns: The "Which" or "That" Dilemma

Pronouns stand for nouns. A particular difficulty, similar to that illustrated by the commas above, concerns the pronouns used for commenting and defining clauses. In "This case should be referred to the coroner's office, which deals with cases of suicide" the "which" clause is a comment and "that" cannot be used. In "The office that deals with suicide cases is the coroner's office", "that" is defining the office.

Verbs: Care with Tenses

Two parts of a verb end in "-ing", the present participle, which acts as an adjective, and the gerund, which acts as a noun. This causes confusion. For example in: "After reviewing the X-rays, the patient had a heart transplant", "reviewing" is an adjective and refers to "patient". The reader is distracted by the unlikely idea that the patient reviewed his own X-rays. On the other hand, in: "Reviewing the X-rays before the heart transplant was a waste of time" "reviewing" is acting as a noun and is part of the subject of "was" and is correctly used. When in doubt, words which end in -ing are easily avoided: "After the surgeon had reviewed the X-rays the patient had a heart transplant" and "It was a waste of time to review the X-rays before the heart transplant".

With regard to tenses, it is a useful convention to put anything that has been done in the past tense and to put general statements in the present tense. When: "After exposure to freezing air the most striking changes were (are) a rise in heart rate and a raised serum cholesterol concentration" is in the past tense it implies that the statement was true in the specific circumstances of the study being reported, but that we do not know if it is always true. The present tense would be used if the author wanted to imply that the statement is true in all circumstances.

The future tense is sometimes used illogically. For example: "In this review some facts about the connections of the globus pallidus will first be summarised." In fact in the review in the journal in front of the reader the facts are summarised (in the present) or, indeed, have been summarised (by the author, in the past). The only question for the future is whether the reader will read the summary.

Another illogical usage is illustrated by: "This paper reports . . ." which implies action by the inanimate paper. What is meant is: "In this paper we report . . . "

One should look critically at all passive verbs to see if they can be rewritten in an active form. The convention that authors are more scientific if they write in the third person is now dying. We now think that: "I first summarise some facts about the globus pallidus" is easier for the reader than: "Some facts about the globus pallidus are first summarised".

Adverbs: Use Correctly

Adverbs tell one more about verbs and to do so an adverb must be put next to its verb, as must adverbial clauses and phrases. Adverbs can be made out of other words by adding "ly" but care is needed. Take the example: "Because the tube and the film are always centred exactly, positioning the patient becomes very simple. More importantly, also routine radiographic views are repeatable." "Always" is correctly placed after "are", and "exactly" is correctly placed after centred but "also" has become separated from its verb (a common occurrence) and should be moved to "are also repeatable". On the other hand, "importantly", an adverbial adaption of the adjective "important", is used fashionably but wrongly as an abbreviation for "what is more important".

If adverbial clusters are used the meaning must be kept clear. For example "The contrast medium was injected quickly manually" sounds odd but the meaning is clear, whereas "The contrast medium was injected three times simultaneously bilaterally" is ambiguous and the author has to be asked what he means.

Prepositions

Prepositions are used to mark a relationship between a noun (or pronoun) and another word. There used to be a rule which itself broke the rule — "do not use a preposition to end a sentence with". We are not interested in this sort of pedantry but we do think that prepositions which imply time (since, while), place (where) and person (who, whose) should be used accurately or replaced with an all-purpose preposition (which, as, if). For example:

"Since all tumours are visible at bronchoscopy, this is the investigation of choice" should be "As all tumours . . . "

"Where the primary tumour can be resected, the prognosis is good" should be "When the primary tumour . . . " or "If the primary tumour . . . "

"Following" should not be used as a preposition because it also has another meaning. "After" is shorter and unambiguous.

Abbreviations: The Bane of Many Readers

Readers hate abbreviations. They have to keep searching back through the paper to remind themselves what each abbreviation means. Some journals rule that a term must be used at least ten times in a paper before an abbreviation is admissible.

Authors love abbreviations. They get tired of writing terms out in full. The critical colleague should be on the side of the reader and insist that abbreviations are eliminated as far as possible.

Numbers

Quite apart from the problems of statistical analysis (see Chap. 7), the critical colleague is on the look out for loose numbers. For example: "25% of all cancer types are curable". Such a statement is often used to start an introduction. This is very distracting because we are not going to believe it unless we are told what cancer types are included in "all", nor are we told the population to which the statement refers — who, where and when. At the very least we must have a reference to the source of this information.

Distraction Removal — An Example

There are more distractions to which critical readers rapidly become sensitised than can be conveyed by isolated grammatical examples. This is exemplified by the imaginary Introduction shown opposite.

In the first version the obvious distractions are in italics (Fig. 5.3). The changes that might be suggested by a subeditor (copy editor, technical editor) without talking to the author are listed in Fig. 5.4 and divided into numbered categories which are listed in Fig. 5.5. These are discussed and then incorporated into the second version (Fig. 5.6).

The second version of the Introduction has then been further amended, after an imaginary face-to-face discussion between the author and a critical colleague, to produce a third version. The third version (Fig. 5.7) incorporates changes which the author confirms to be correct but which the subeditor could not make for fear of changing the meaning or introducing inaccuracies, or because he did not know what the author meant.

Experimental studies with intrathecal dextropomorpho-editate antimony

A Jones and B Smith

Introduction

At the present time it is believed (Jones and Smith 1981) that *approximately* 150 ml of intravenous dextropomorpho-editate antimony *(IvDEA) is required* for the treatment of each severe case of panacetate encephalitis, but adverse reactions are numerous.

After treatment *commences* the *vast majority* of patients *demonstrate skin rashes* and *complain of intractable pruritus* and the skin *comparatively* frequently becomes purple *in colour due to the fact* that *IvDEA* contains traces of laevopomorpho-editate antimony *(LEA)*. The *literature shows* that the *serum LEA* is *persistently elevated in excess of* 0.8 micrograms ml *throughout the duration of the skin lesion. It is also possible* that the blood supply to the *epidermis* is *significantly* decreased, especially in *female subjects*.

Brown et al (1982) are *of the same opinion* but, having had some experience of other forms of encephalitis, they *anticipate* that intrathecal DEA (ItDEA) will *be of assistance* to a wider *spectrum* of patients *at some future time*.

In this unfortunate therapeutic situation it seemed to the present researchers that, *as already stated*, more *sophisticated* forms of DEA therapy could be developed. *They theorised* that *sacrificing various* laboratory animals *following* ItDEA would *reveal data* about the *externalisation* of DEA across the brain/blood barrier.

This *communication reports* the results in . . .

(205 words)

Fig. 5.3. Removal of distractions: Introduction — version 1.

Version 1: Distractions (numbers refer to types)	**Suggested changes: see version 2**
1 At the present time	delete
1 it is believed	delete
2 approximately	about
3 IvDEA	intravenous dextropomorpho-editate antimony
1,4 is required	are needed
1 commences	begins, starts
1 vast majority'	most
5 demonstrate	develop (it happens to the patient)
6 skin rashes	rashes

Fig. 5.4. List of distractions removed from Introduction (*continued overleaf*)

1,5	complain of intractable pruritus	complain of itching (patients' words)
1	comparatively	delete (compared with what?)
1,6	in colour	delete (purple can be nothing else)
1	due to the fact	because
3	IvDEA	intravenous dextropomorpho-editate antimony
7	literature shows	which literature? reference(s) please
8	serum LEA	the concentration (micrograms/ml) in the serum
6	persistently	delete
1	elevated	delete (raised)
1	in excess of	above
1	throughout the duration of the in lesion	while the rash lasts
1	It is also possible	may
9	epidermis	is epidermis meant? or is this an elegant variation for skin?
2	significantly	change — a technical word in statistics
1	female subjects	women
1,4	of the same opinion	agreed (past — they did it in 1982)
5	anticipate (implies action)	expected (also past tense)
1	be of assistance	help
2	spectrum	change — a technical term in optics
1,6	at some future time	delete (implied by 'would')
1	In this unfortunate therapeutic situation	delete
1	it seemed to the present researchers	we thought
1,6	as already stated	delete
5	sophisticated	change — derived from the ancient Greek sect of Sophists who used any argument, however fallacious, to support their case
1	They	we
10	theorised	argued
5	sacrificing	killed (no ritual implications)
7	various	specify which
5	following	after
5	reveal	change — too strong, not a revelation
1	data	facts
10	externalisation	be more specific
1	communication	paper, article
4	reports	we report — a communication is inanimate

Fig. 5.4. (*continued*)

```
 1 = pompous verbiage — delete, simplify or make active   (23)
 2 = technical word used out of its field                 ( 3)
 3 = abbreviation — irritating for the reader             ( 2)
 4 = wrong grammar                                        ( 3)
 5 = inaccurate or misleading use of a word               ( 7)
 6 = redundant word(s)                                    ( 5)
 7 = factually imprecise                                  ( 2)
 8 = technically imprecise                                ( 1)
 9 = is it an "elegant variation" or not?                 ( 1)
10 = unnecessary neologism                                ( 2)
```

Fig. 5.5. Types and numbers of distractions removed from version 1.

Experimental studies with intrathecal dextropomorpho-editate antimony

A Jones and B Smith

Introduction

About 150 ml of intravenous dextropomorpho-editate antimony are needed for the treatment of each severe case of panacetate encephalitis (Jones and Smith 1981), but adverse reactions are numerous.

After treatment begins most patients develop rashes and complain of itching and the skin frequently becomes purple, because dextropomorpho-editate antimony contains traces of laevopomorpho-editate antimony. The concentration of laevopomorpho-editate antimony in the serum is above 0.8 micrograms/ml while the rash lasts (reference). The blood supply to the skin may be less than normal, especially in women.

Brown et al (1982) agreed but, having had experience of other forms of encephalitis, they expected that intrathecal dextropomorpho-editate antimony would help a wider range of patients.

We thought that better dextropomorpho-editate antimony therapy could be developed. We argued that killing rats and guinea pigs after giving dextropomorpho-editate antimony intrathecally would tell us whether dextropomorpho-editate antimony could escape across the brain/blood barrier.

In this paper we report the results in . . .

(154 words)

Fig. 5.6. Version 2 of Introduction after removal of distractions.

Fig. 5.7. Final version 3 of Introduction.

1. Pompous Verbiage

This is the commonest type of distraction. It consists of extra words put
in to make the writing sound more important. Authors sometimes have
reasons for being pompous, and may justifiably be pompous on purpose, but they should not be pompous unconsciously or unintentionally.
All the superfluous words have to be cleared away to discover the
meaning, just as one clears weeds off a tombstone to see the inscription.

2. Technical Word Used Out of Its Field

Some words, such as "approximately", "significantly" and "spectrum"
have precise technical meanings, as in statistics and optics. If technical

words are not used precisely they lose their precision. If something more general is meant, such a word should be changed to a more general one.

3. Abbreviation

Abbreviations are convenient for authors but irritate readers, particularly those unfamiliar with the subject. It is therefore courteous to use abbreviations as rarely as possible.

4. Wrong Grammar

i)   The subject of "is required", "150 ml" (an acceptable abbreviation for "millilitres"?), is plural.

ii)   Brown et al. *were* of the same opinion when they wrote in 1982. The reader does not know if they are still of the same opinion. They also "anticipated" in the past.

iii)   Reporting has to be done by a person.

5. Inaccurate or Misleading Use of Words

i)   A demonstrator might demonstrate the rash to the students. The patient is most unlikely to do so, although he might be persuaded to show it to them. Familiarity with this sort of pompous writing makes it fairly certain that all that is meant is that "most patients develop rashes".

ii)   It is very unlikely that a complaining patient, even a complaining doctor, would say "This intractable pruritus is driving me mad".

iii)   "Anticipate" implies action, as in "The pilot anticipated the crash by swerving away from the rocks". Brown et al. did not, as far as the reader can tell, intend to do anything, so "expected" is more accurate. The reader is then not distracted by wondering what Brown et al. might have been thinking of doing.

iv)   "Sophisticated" is often used pompously to mean "smart" or "trendy" or "up to date" or even "advanced", as was presumably meant here. Most authors are shocked by the idea that they are using any argument, however fallacious, to support their case. Even when that is true, it is not usually what authors mean to say.

v)   "Sacrifice" has overtones of ritual and religion, and the word is used to make "killing" acceptable to sentimental readers. To many other readers it adds sentiment and inaccuracy.

vi) "Following" is ambiguous here. It could be the present participle (verb-adjective) telling us more about "animals" and meaning "walking behind" them. As a preposition, "after" is less ambiguous.

vii) "Reveal" is too strong a word. The authors merely hoped to find something out.

6. Redundant Word(s)

This is unnecessary repetition, exemplified by "skin rashes" and "purple in colour". What other types of rash are there? Can purple be other than a colour? "Persistently" repeats "throughout the duration". These are further examples of extra words which may help to convey spoken messages but which impede written messages.

7. Factually Imprecise

With "literature" and "various", the reader would be helped by more precise information, the lack of which he suspects is due to laziness on the part of the author.

8. Technically Imprecise

The "serum laevopomorpho-editate antimony" is a lazy colloquial expression for the "concentration of laevopomorpho-editate antimony in the serum", which is actually given (0.8 micrograms/ml). "Level" is an imprecise word often used instead of the specific technical word "concentration".

9. Is It an "Elegant Variation" or Not?

Synonyms and elegant variations, which are often not exact synonyms, are used when authors think that it is not "literary" to use the same word or phrase repeatedly. The reader of scientific papers wastes time wondering whether the author has varied the word or phrase to convey a different meaning or for the "literary" reason.

For example, we know that the blood supply to the skin is in the dermis and not in the epidermis, so it is likely that "epidermis" is being used as an elegant variation for "skin". The reader would get on more quickly if "skin" were used each time, and would not mind if the writing were less elegant.

10. Unnecessary Neologism

It is not necessary to create a verb out of the noun "theory" or a noun out of the adjective "external" if words to express the required meanings already exist. In the latter case the use of a new word whose meaning is not clear is itself distracting.

The Final Version After Removal of Distraction

In the discussion between the critical colleague and the authors of the second version (Fig. 5.6) the following points could be established, and the final version (Fig. 5.7) of the Introduction then written.

1. The adverse reactions were numerous in the sense that they occurred in many of the patients and not in the sense that there were many different adverse reactions. Indeed a new reference which covered the rashes, itching and discolouration, as well as attributing them all to the laevopomorpho-editate antimony, was found. It was agreed that "side-effects" was a less pompous term than "adverse reactions". "After treatment begins" was redundant because the side-effects could not occur before the drug had been given.

2. It was thought useful to say that the side-effects occurred in association with a known concentration of laevopomorpho-editate antimony in the serum, but it also emerged that the corresponding concentrations in the tissues, such as the skin, were not known.

3. The point about the blood supply was not relevant to this introduction, although it might be relevant in the discussion.

4. Jones and Smith wished to acknowledge that they got the idea of giving dextropomorpho-editate antimony intrathecally from Brown et al. (1982). The rest of that paper was not relevant here.

5. Jones and Smith set out to test the intrathecal idea in rats and guinea pigs (Why those species? Not relevant here, see the methods section). It did in fact involve killing the rats and guinea pigs (with the approval of the ethical committee) but that also appears in the methods section and need not be mentioned in the introduction.

6. When the message had been clarified it was agreed that the title gave too little information. The new title did imply that the substances were detected extrathecally, but the authors and indeed the rest of the article confirmed that that was so. "Administration" was rather pompous but fitted better here than the "doses" used in the text. Is this a type 9 distraction?

The Word Processor

This chapter was written on a microcomputer using a word processing program. Undoubtedly microcomputers and word processing programs — the "new technology" — have a great deal to offer medical and scientific writers because with them it is so simple to remove ambiguities and distractions (as one writes and on reflection), and for creative writing they are the best invention since the quill pen. Provided the author can type a little (and he can easily learn from a home tutor or cassette course), this way of writing has four advantages over the old-fashioned pen and paper method.

Firstly, when one types directly onto the screen it is so easy to move the words, punctuation, sentences and paragraphs around that the result is much more precise than can be achieved by making insertions and deletions on paper. Indeed, the paper format inhibits trial and error whereas the screen format positively encourages it.

Secondly, one can have a fresh double-spaced printed copy at will and be completely independent of any secretary or typist. At any stage one can give one's colleague a fresh double-spaced printed copy on which to make his suggestions, knowing how easy it is to incorporate any agreed changes with minimal retyping.

Thirdly, the avoidance of retyping means that, while mistakes can easily be removed, new mistakes are not written in. This is particularly useful for references.

Lastly, the disc or tape on which the writing is stored can be sent to the editor for editing and then to the printer for computer typesetting, thus further reducing the risks of introducing errors and reducing the amount of typing.

Conclusions

In this chapter we have endeavoured to establish a method with which one can systematically and constructively criticise scientific articles, one's own or other people's, at any stage. It is used to identify the author's message and also to detect and remove ambiguities and distractions of different types so that the reader may receive the message in the shortest time and with the least effort. Authors cannot afford to forget that for most readers nowadays medical reading is work, partly because there is so much of it and partly because there are usually so many ambiguities and distractions. These not only obscure the message, but also make it difficult to assess the validity of the results and their interpretation.

References

Altman DG (1980). Statistics and ethics in medical research. Misuse of statistics is unethical. Br Med J 2:1182–1184

Bradford Hill A (1965). The reasons for writing. Br Med J 2:870

Garfield E (1982). The ethics of scientific publication: authorship attribution and citation amnesia. Current Contents 25:6–10

Gowers E (1962). The complete plain words. Pelican Books, Harmondsworth

Gowers E (1968). Fowler's modern English usage, 2nd edn, revised by Sir Ernest Gowers. Oxford University Press, Oxford

International Committee of Medical Journal Editors (1982) Uniform requirements for manuscripts submitted to biomedical journals. Br Med J 284:1766–1770

Okada S, Ohtsuki, H, Midorikawa O, Hashimoto K (1982). Bronchial plasmacytoma identified by immunoperoxidase technique on paraffin embedded section. Acta Pathol Jpn, 32:149–155

World Medical Association (1964). Human experimentation. Code of ethics of the World Medical Association. Br Med J 2:177

Further Reading

Lloyd SM (ed) (1982) Roget's thesaurus of English words and phrases. Longman, Harlow

O'Connor M, Woodford FP (1975) Writing scientific papers in English. Associated Scientific Publishers, Amsterdam

Parkinson JE (1971) A manual of English for the overseas doctor. Churchill Livingstone, Edinburgh Harlow New York

Whale J (1984) Put it in writing. J M Dent and Sons, London

6. Illustrating Talks and Articles

Marco Sorgi and Clifford Hawkins

One picture is worth more than ten thousand words.

Ancient Chinese proverb

[Valuable as they are, illustrations are seldom worth quite so much! They do, however, complement a talk and enhance a book, aiding comprehension and relieving the monotony of continuous text. The Editors]

ILLUSTRATING TALKS

Scientists, businessmen and politicians all need to present their ideas and work to audiences who are either familiar or unfamiliar with their subject. The main object of the message is always "to be understood". Apparently we remember 20% of what we hear, 30% of what we see, but between 50% and 75% of what we both see and hear. It has also been stated that we learn 12% of what we know from hearing and 80% through written material — through our eyes. Life today — through advertising, television and design of books — is based on these facts. The audio-visual presentation is regarded as the best method of holding the attention of the public. This combined use of the two systems clarifies the meaning of an idea, it imprints the message in the memory of the audience, gives better support to scientific or artistic points and certainly makes the time that the public or audience attend any lecture more interesting and bearable.

The advances in technology in presenting mass messages through movies, television, visual advertising, colour codes, voice and auditory perception have been revolutionary. One result is that visual messages, television and film, have a much faster timing than just a generation ago; proof of this is that when we nowadays see an old movie we often find it boring, mainly because the speed and the aggressiveness of the image and sound have been surpassed: it moves too slowly! We have been taught to absorb messages at a faster speed, but in order to absorb those messages quicker, we need a higher degree of sensory stimulation through a better matching of colours, images and sounds. When a speaker delivers a message today he is competing in the subconscious of the audience with the brightness of advertising messages and with highly matched and carefully conducted visual studies. Hence the need to use all the technical advantages in an audio-visual presentation. Spoken words and images have to be in harmony and complementary, without repetition or contradictions: the words will explain and support the visual image and the visual image will clarify and reinforce the spoken message. A successful talk depends upon precise words, clearly pronounced and with suitable emphasis — as are or should be employed by professional speakers. Illustrations must be easily recognisable with appropriate colours and pleasant to look at; the information on any slide must support the lecturer's spoken word. Audiences are becoming more aware of the qualities of a good speaker and of a good slide and are less tolerant of a bad speaker and poor visual aids.

Script of Your Talk

Most speakers start by preparing a script of their communication; the messages which are intended to be put over to the audience are pinpointed and arranged in chronological sequence. The alternative of choosing a few slides and using them as visual aids to improvise a talk is an amateurish approach which can be successful only when practised by very experienced and bright speakers.

Bear in mind the nature of your audience when constructing the script; in medicine there may be — in the same auditorium — a medical student, a doctor in training, a staff member and an experienced and senior professional. A good speaker will work hard to make his talk comprehensible to all. If, as is likely, you are an expert on the topic (otherwise you probably would not be doing this), you do not need to confuse the issue or show that you know a lot about the subject, thinking that by doing so you will impress the audience. The best way to show that you know what you are talking about is by *simplifying* the issue in a way that your message will come across to the audience clearly and that it will be remembered.

A Timetable for Preparing Your Talk

Producing a 15-second TV commercial can cost $2000 per second, with thousands of man hours of work invested in it. A 100-minute film can cost $50,000,000 and hundreds of thousands of man hours of work. Most good medical speakers find that they spend at least 10 times more time in preparation than they had anticipated. A timetable can be prepared bearing in mind the sequence of what has to be done:

● Write the script
● Define the content of each slide
● Type the slide
● Construct graphics, tables and figures
● Photograph the artwork
● Assemble a group for rehearsal
● Do the rehearsals

Allow 3–5 days for things that can — and will — go wrong. Also fix the rehearsal for 7–10 days before the talk so that there is time for alteration of any slides.

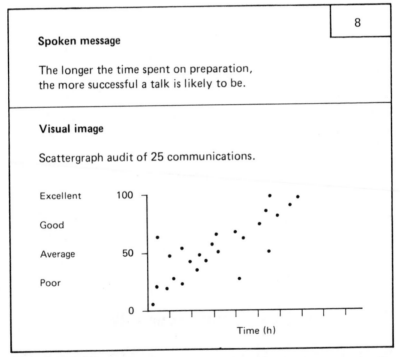

Fig. 6.1. Record card with message of the slide (*top half*) and visual image to use for slide (*bottom half*).

Constructing Your Talk

The script provides the source for preparing slides. One method is to use record cards (10 × 15 cm; 4 × 6 in.): the top half can be used to write the point or message of that slide and the bottom half for a rough drawing of the visual image that you want to use (Fig. 6.1). The card is numbered in the top right corner, using one number for each message; if more than one image is needed for a particular message, the card can be coded with the same number plus a letter, i.e. 3a, 3b, 3c etc. These cards will make it easier to rehearse the talk, and changes in the sequence can be made if necessary. At this stage, the more time spent in planning the cards, the more time will be saved in designing slides and the talk itself. When you have finished building up your card sequence, it is often helpful to discuss the talk with a colleague or a senior member of the department as criticism or comments may save you wasting time. Rehearsing a talk with your wife, or husband if you are a woman scientist, can also be valuable as ideas have to be expressed simply — and it is usually the jargon surrounding an idea rather than the idea itself which confuses the listener.

Slides

The slide is still the most important visual aid and will remain so in spite of the increasing use of other methods in teaching, such as the overhead projector, cinematography and television. The incomprehensible or unnecessary slide, however, wastes the speaker's time and oppresses the audience. Each slide needs careful thought and should speak for itself simply and clearly.

The Purpose of Slides

Slides may make or mar a communication. Their main purpose is to illustrate aspects of a talk which are more easily understood by pictures. This statement may seem trite but slides may befog rather than illuminate. They may also be used to guide the speaker as well as the audience, acting as visual prompters that remind him of the major points of his talks. Indeed, he may then expound his subject by simply commenting on the slides — a method preferable to reading from typescript. Some speakers like to keep prints of their slides in their notes and this saves them turning to look at their slides except for just checking by a glance that the right slide has been projected.

Slides should not be used just to embellish a lecture except for an occasional amusing or decorative slide which is very helpful in keeping an audience interested, variety and surprise being introduced to an otherwise monotonous subject. There should always be some reason for showing a slide, even though slides have become such a traditional feature of every communication.

Bad Slides

Some slides are used to cram in detail which cannot, from lack of time, be spoken. So 10 or 20 lines of figures or writing may be packed in, being the outcome of months of preparation and needing an hour or so of study to understand. Such overcrowded slides, which often resemble a page from a railway timetable, were probably unknown in the days when speakers had to make their own slides. Now, with the aid of mechanical methods, there is no limit as to what can be printed on a slide; hence great blocks of letterpress are projected, 30 seconds or less being allotted for each slide, often hardly legible, to be seen. Speakers continue to show these futile slides, either from thoughtlessness or to impress the audience with all their evidence. Unfortunately, the audience is either bewildered or bored. Some may find solace in closing their eyes and just listening, as the meaning of a talk may then become clear. Few lectures require experimental details or the minutiae of results, and these should be omitted.

The temptation to use illustrations composed of tabular matter taken from articles and books must be resisted, for these are usually unsuitable for projection unless simplified or converted into graphs or histograms.

Legibility

No slide should be shown unless it can be read by the back row of the audience. A simple way of ensuring this is to provide lettering on the slide which is large enough to be read by the naked eye without projection; this also makes it much easier to sort the slide before a lecture. Another way is to make sure that the lettering, before being made into a slide, is large enough to be read from a distance of 2 metres (6 feet).

How to Present Data on Slides

Any data for making into slides have to be prepared especially for that purpose. Graphs, tables and figures used for publication have a very different lay out because it is assumed that the reader will spend as much time as he needs to understand each illustration. By contrast, with a slide it is the speaker who decides how much time to use for explaining the data. A figure for publication can contain data that the reader will extract from it; in contrast the main purpose of a slide is to convey a message. In order to deliver one clear message per slide, you have to follow these guidelines:

- Select the information
- Synthesise the idea
- Simplify the data

A slide does not need to contain all the information because the speaker will explain details to the audience. All materials must be scrutinized to find the best way of showing it pictorially, such as by a graph, histogram or diagram. Statistical data, such as columns of figures and tables, can be converted into a picture showing relationships and trends, to illustrate ideas derived from the data. The design should be simple and open with plenty of space, for its contents should not only be clearly visible but also must be grasped easily during its brief appearance on the screen. Its meaning should be obvious without explanation.

Content of a Slide

Slides can be designs based on the following characteristics:

- Text
- Data: represented by tables of numbers, charts or diagrams
- Drawings
- Pictures: represented by patients, operations, pathological specimens or by allegories that stress a message.

A rule to be kept in mind is that the message and your slide should never mislead the audience. Do not try to make your data appear better than they are just to produce a fancy slide. Slides should usually be oblong rather than vertical — landscape rather than portrait (Fig. 6.2); the former fit the screen better and avoid the bottom of the slide being projected off the screen. So the dimensions of artwork have to be produced with a ratio between height and width of 2 to 3; this is the same as the shape of the film slides (20 mm × 36 mm).

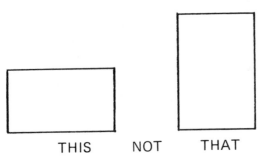

THIS   NOT   THAT

Fig. 6.2. Shape of slide.

Text

Lettering should be limited to about three or four lines, and should never be more than seven, including the title. If you have too much on one slide, turn it into two.

The electric golfball or daisy wheel typewriter provides a quick and easy method of doing the lettering, which will be free from irregularities, sharply outlined and perfectly aligned; larger lettering can be obtained by using a larger typehead. However, lettering from an ordinary typewriter can be entirely satisfactory (Fig. 6.3). To prevent the fuzzy appearance so common on typed slides, the keys must be scrupulously cleaned. Typing should be as black as possible on good quality pure white paper. Some recommend using a new fabric ribbon and reversing the carbon paper so that the carbon surface faces the undersurface of the paper, or replacing the usual ribbon by a carbon ribbon or sheet of carbon paper. Special ribbons made of cellulose acetate can be fitted to certain typewriters and give a clearer outline to letters. Other methods include stencil lettering, dry transfer instant lettering, printing through an IBM composer or photocomposing. Generally, lower case letters, — the small letters of the alphabet (so called because of their original position in the compositor case) — are easier to read than capitals. This is hardly surprising as the eye is more accustomed to the former in newspapers and books.

Slides are easily prepared as negatives, white lettering on a black background, instead of the customary positive, black lettering on white. A neat and attractive appearance is given by a black background, for dust and minor scratches do not show. Dazzle is avoided by lines and letters not being too thick, or by colours. It is simple for the photographer to brush over letters or lines of diagrams with water-soluble dyes (photo tints). The same colour should be used for data derived from the same source. Very bright colours must be avoided because they may appear to scintillate like stained-glass windows, impairing readability. Dark greens or blues are unsatisfactory as they darken the room; reds

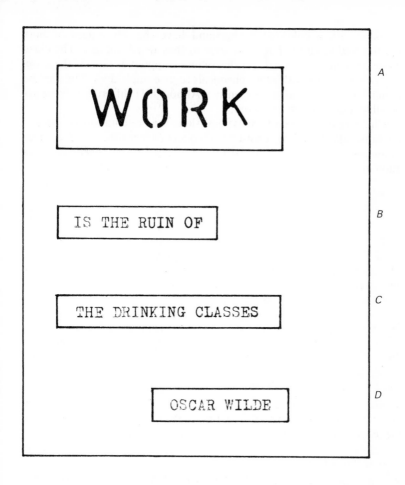

Fig. 6.3. Lettering for slides. *A*, stencil; *B*, electric typewriter; *C*, ordinary typewriter with special care; *D* ordinary typewriter.

and yellows are better "eye catchers" than blues, and when a line is coloured blue, it should be drawn thicker to allow more penetration of light. Disadvantages are that pointers other than the illuminated type cannot readily be used and there is no obvious "frame" to confine the attention of the audience — and darkness makes it difficult to make notes.

Black letters on white make it easier for the audience to take notes as the room need not be darkened and it has been suggested that those with a refractory error may read them more easily, as contraction of the iris improves the focusing power of the eye: however lettering should always be large enough for anyone, unless suffering from severe visual impairment, to see.

117

Slides with a coloured background have the advantages of both positive and negative slides and none of their disadvantages. The diazo process is commonly used, for diazonium compounds possess the property of combining with other chemicals to give stable dyes. The method requires little skill and is inexpensive. Although 11 different colours are possible, blue is often preferred.

Whatever the choice of the type of slide, the presentation of slides in the same talk should be consistent. Frequent changes from dark to clear slides will prevent the vision becoming adapted to any particular situation and may cause fatigue.

Data

The data should stimulate the interest of the audience rather than just giving specific details and accurate numbers to decimal points. They can be presented in various ways:

● Tables or column charts can be used to compare different groups. Tables should be limited to four columns and four horizontal lines. Shading can be used to differentiate one column from another and preferably columns are separated by a space rather larger than their own width. A particular result can be written in bolder lettering or colours.

● Bar charts (Fig. 6.4) can be used to illustrate comparisons between groups in the same way as in a column chart. Horizontal bars may make the lettering easier (Fig. 6.5). Limit the number of bars to five or seven, and state the code in the upper right corner and the scale of numbers used at the bottom.

● Pie charts can be used to illustrate the division of a whole into different parts (Fig. 6.6). A useful rule is to limit the number of slices to five and to place percentages and numbers inside the pie and the labels and descriptions of each one of the slices outside.

● Line graphs are used to express changing relations when they occur in relation to time. Put the scale on the left margin and the time scale on the bottom. Limit the number of curves to three or four and distinguish each by different symbols or line design; normal values should also be inserted when they are necessary. The scale used to measure must be put clearly, also the zero point on the axis and any break in the continuity of the line should be indicated.

● Scatter diagrams illustrate the degree of correlation or distribution in compared groups.

● Flow charts are important in describing successive stages of a disease or procedure.

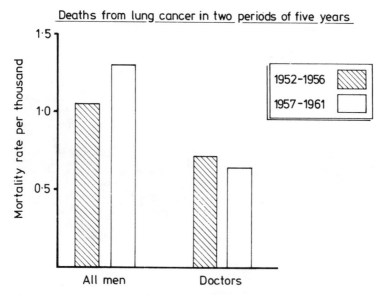

Fig 6.4. Vertical bar chart to illustrate comparisons between two groups.

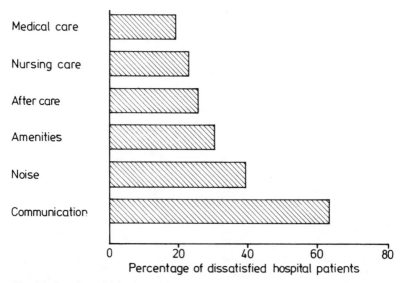

Fig. 6.5. Bar chart with horizontal bars.

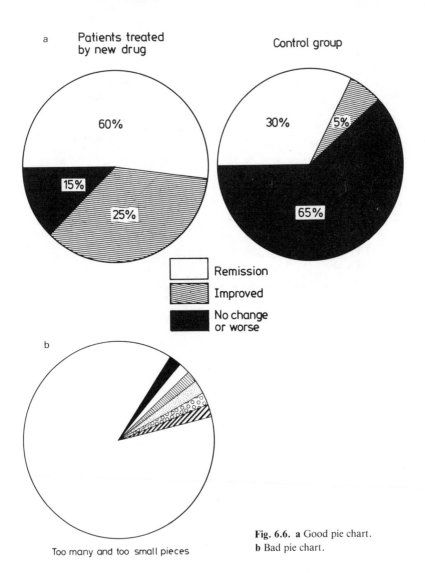

a Patients treated by new drug

Control group

60%

15%

25%

30%

5%

65%

Remission

Improved

No change or worse

b

Too many and too small pieces

Fig. 6.6. a Good pie chart.
b Bad pie chart.

Drawings

These are usually done as line or tonal drawings. Thicker lines are usually used than for lettering. Sketches can be used to explain a real picture or be placed adjacent to a radiograph.

Pictures

Pictures must be clear and not overcrowded with information. A picture may consist of a photograph, an ECG, an X-ray, a gamma scan, an anatomical specimen, bacteriological plates, an insect leg or a surgical procedure. The attention of the audience should be directed to a specific point without the need of a pointer. X-rays should be cropped of any unnecessary bits, and an arrow can be put on to demonstrate a salient point.

An amusing or illustrated picture can also be inserted into a talk, a simple example being that if discussion is about a cold temperature, a piece of ice could be shown. However, always be sure to exercise good taste, especially with humour. Remember that each image could arouse different feelings and reactions depending on the culture, background and personality of the audience. The same message which can be enjoyed and easily understood by one audience, might be totally rejected by another. As an example, the speaker might say ". . . it is important to work as a team for the benefit of the patient". In Texas, USA, a picture of the Astros, the local football team, might amusingly illustrate the spoken message. The same picture might not have the same effect elsewhere in the world.

Slides of Operations

The surgeon has to instruct the photographer exactly as to what is wanted — the orientation, the size of the field of view and the focus of attention. The structures have to be clearly exposed, visible and recognisable. Great care has to be taken in cleaning the photographic field of view of undesired material: dirty sponges, unused instruments, blood or débris. Clean the gloves and retractors with a sponge and dry the surgical field. Apply clean towels around the field of view and make sure that shadows from other organs, hands or instruments do not mask important areas. Devoting a few minutes to these details will make all the difference between a good slide which will be useful for many years and another that will look sloppy.

Pictures of pathological specimens and other objects are better obtained in the studio than in real life conditions.

The Making of Slides

Professional Help — Or Do It Yourself

Those who have access to a professional medical illustrator are fortunate: all that they need to do is to draw their pictures roughly, *discuss them with him*, and he will do the rest — hopefully smothering at birth any railway timetable slides.

Many, however, have to make illustrations themselves. Some departments of medical illustration provide facilities for anyone to come and use the equipment and work in the department itself. This happens at the Royal Postgraduate Medical School in London and all technical details are clearly described and illustrated in *Presentation of Data in Science* by Linda Reynolds and Doig Simmonds (1981), which covers everything from paper and pencil to useful gadgets such as the transilluminated drawing board (Rotaboard).

"Do-It-Yourself" Slides

You can produce your own slides if you have the skill and the equipment and, with modern technology, such slides can be of high quality. You need a 35-mm camera with appropriate lens system, a stand to hold the camera, a light source that will not produce shadows, and the appropriate films. After the pictures are taken, the film can be processed either by a photographic laboratory or by yourself. A home system is the polaroid new development film for colour transparency films or black and white (high contrast and continuous tone); this can be used in any 35-mm camera and developed in 1 minute so that you have your slides mounted and ready in a very short time.

An automatic copier and slide processor called the AUTODIA KV 3030 can be bought (The Projectina Company Ltd, Skelmorlie, Ayrshire, Scotland). This produces a monochrome 35-mm slide from an original in only 40 seconds and each slide is cheap. Lettering is typed, preferably with a small dense type face; a form of zoom lens allows adjustment of this to the dimensions of the slide. Graphs, line drawings and bar or other charts can also be copied but colour, such as for the diazo slide, is not possible. The film is "fixed" in 2 seconds and the finished slide has a mount.

The Professional Slide

When facilities are available, it is best to leave the preparation, photography and development of your pictures to professionals as the outcome will certainly be better. Do, however, show consideration for the staff of the department as much of their time can be wasted by requests for useless slides (Hawkins and Dee 1973). Consulting the department before work is requested saves everyone time, and advice is usually freely available, though sometimes in practice the individual thinks that he knows better. Guidance may be needed on how much to put on a slide, how to design it, the pros and cons of black and white and so on. Work should be vetted at all stages of production and the typescript for slides should be corrected with the same care as is given to proofs for an article, *before* being photographed; the original can be retained in the speaker's notes to save him turning to look at the screen. Most users of the photographic department are considerate but some, especially the inexperienced who are naturally ambitious to deliver a paper, can make unreasonable demands, as in any service department. For example, a dozen or more slides may be demanded for a talk in 48 hours time, although the speaker has had 6 months to prepare it. The time needed for completing different requests varies: 7–10 days is the minimum time required for prints or slides of tables, drawings, graphs and X-rays; 3–4 days are necessary for clinical and routine photographs in monochrome and 7 days if these are needed in colour; and 6–8 weeks are needed to produce cine film. Request cards must be filled in completely so that the photographer has a clear idea of what should be photographed.

Technical Points

Mounts

Mounts differ in materials, closure systems, surface protection, thickness and cost. The plastic bound one is most widely used and has the advantage that it is slim and does not bend. Some contain glass to protect the film. Metallic frames have the advantage that they do not wear out, but they are thick and heavy. Cardboard mounts are inexpensive but are sometimes too thick and if bent can jam the projector. The window on a slide can vary in size: the usual standard size is $36 \text{ mm} \times 24 \text{ mm}$, though another window, the superslide, is $50 \text{ mm} \times 50 \text{ mm}$.

Labelling Slides

The exact method of labelling slides must be clear to the projectionist. The international convention calls for a spot to be placed in the lower left-hand corner as the slide is viewed by the naked eye; this will be visible at the upper right corner when the slide is inserted. Colour "spot" labels are useful for filing and sorting slides. Many number their slides as well as marking them; this helps to prevent the anti-climax of the last slide being shown first and may be useful in the discussion afterwards, for the speaker may wish to refer to one of them or to any reserve slides; furthermore if the projectionist drops them, they can be assembled at once in the right order. The numbering of slides should also be put in the notes. The slide box must be labelled with the speaker's name; it is also helpful to put an arrow at the start of the slides and to indicate that dimmed lighting and not complete blackout should generally be used.

Storage of Slides

When choosing a method of storing slides, consider the following requirements: it should be easy to handle (with easy access for reviewing slides), cheap and easy to keep.

A good method is the filing cabinet with suspension filing plastic sheets (Fig. 6.7). Depending on their size, each page will contain between 20 and 24 slides that are easy to see and a standard cabinet could store up to 1500 slides. The same system of plastic transparent pages with pockets that can be stored in loose-leaf binders is available but the disadvantage

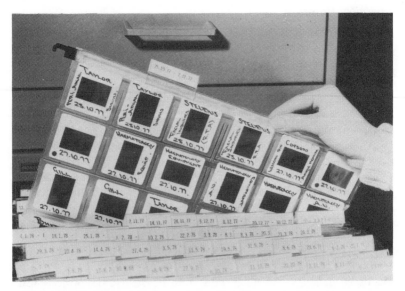

Fig. 6.7. Filing cabinet with suspension filing plastic sheets.

is that slides cannot easily be reviewed and the weight of the slide may bend the page — unless the binder is stored vertically.

Sorting and Viewing Slides

This can be done on a light box or viewer. The viewer can be as simple as an X-ray viewing box lying on its side, or a homemade box can be made of any size needed: paint white on the inside of the box, use a good light bulb and cover the top with a white plastic surface. Usually the standard carousel tray holds 80 slides so your sorter could have a similar capacity. This type of viewer makes it easy to assemble slides for a talk and this is especially simple if lettering is large enough to be read without magnification or projection — just by the naked eye.

Transporting Slides

Slides can be transported to the meeting either in plastic boxes (they may break if dropped) but these have the disadvantage that it is difficult to review the slides without taking them out. So a better way is to transport the slides in plastic file transparent sheets which can be opened and slides examined anywhere without any special lighting conditions. If you are travelling by plane, carry the slides in your briefcase with you. One distinguished speaker who travelled to the other side of the world and left his slides with the luggage found that he had arrived without them.

The Perfect Slide

The perfect slide needs little or no explanation. Preferably it should be designed so that the speaker does not have to point or look at it except to check that it is the correct one. Reference can be made to the red or dotted line, or to the part shown by an arrow. If text slides are being explained, the same key words should be used when speaking as in the slide itself. If, heaven forbid, you have an abbreviation on your slide, explain it unless it is one in common use.

A frequent fault is to have too many slides and to show them too quickly. The number of slides that are going to be shown in the allotted time should have been established during the writing of the script and checked during the rehearsal. Obviously the total number depends on the time needed for each slide to be seen and this varies greatly.

Avoid old slides used many times before unless an old slide is presented to stress a point, remarking on the fact, for example, that "it is the original slide of 20 years ago". Avoid the temptation to insert slides in a communication just because you have them. Blank or interval slides are useful when the subject is being changed or when the speaker is going to spend some minutes just talking without the distraction of a slide; a plain diazo slide can be used for this. A test slide is often useful at the start to allow the projectionist to check focusing, especially if the first slide of the lecture is a surprise one — otherwise the surprise will be lost on the audience.

Visual presentations, as with any scientific material, are protected by copyright. If anyone else's data are included, the source must be acknowledged, usually at the bottom of the slide. If data are modified, you should quote also the name and source but state that it is "modified from" or "from".

Helpful "dont's" include the following:

● Never skip a slide: if the talk has been properly prepared and timed by rehearsals, there should be no need to say "well, let's skip this one because . . ." If it is not important, it should not be there.

● Avoid going back to the previous slide. If there is need to emphasise the message, have a copy inserted in the right position.

● Never say "this slide looks complicated".

● Never say "I apologise for the poor legibility and quality of this slide".

● Never lend a slide even to your closest friend as, like lending a book, it is unlikely to be returned. If you are asked for one, take the name and address of the requestant, make a copy and send it with your regards. This will always be less expensive than losing the slide.

Projectors

There are two types of projector, the linear and the circular tray (carousel). Preferably load your slides yourself, making sure that each is properly orientated with a dot in the upper right corner. There is a risk of losing the last slide in the carousel type as it may not have reappeared in the tray.

Two projectors can be used on a parallel, one by the side of the other, using two screens. The real usefulness of this is when you want to show changes that are difficult unless they are compared side by side. This may apply to radiographs, such as those depicting the healing of a gastric ulcer. Also, tables can be presented on one screen and as a matching image on the other one. The audience must be given time to look at both. The blank pause between slides can be avoided by using two or more projectors on one screen with a "dissolve unit" which switches one on gradually and meanwhile switches off the other one. Some projectors even allow slides to be changed so fast that a cinematographic effect is produced.

ILLUSTRATING ARTICLES

An illustration is defined by the printer as any material which cannot be set in type: photographs, line drawings, charts, graphs, tracings and so on. All these are called figures. Tables, which are set in type, are just called tables; these are useful for extracting boring material from the script and for comparing two sets of figures.

Each illustration should be worth the space which is occupied and must fulfil a special purpose; none should repeat material already presented in the text or tables. However, data in tables or histograms should be capable of re-analysis by the reader.

There are various methods of illustrating facts or ideas and the most suitable one should be chosen. A drawing or photograph already made for another purpose is often unsatisfactory to use for publication as it may lack the special qualities required.

Line Drawings

A pure white, blue-white or pale blue background is necessary for line drawings as this reflects the maximum amount of light in contrast to the black lines of the drawing. Bristol board proofing paper or CS10 is particularly suitable for pen and ink work; pure white paper is satisfactory provided it is not fibrous or spongy. The ink should be dense black Indian ink of waterproof type. The printing process for line work is only capable of recording black *or* white so that all lines must be pure black without thinning into grey; a grey line will either appear black or disappear altogether. Greys are produced by cross-hatching and stippling areas. However, a black-and-white illustration can have "tones" added to it without increasing the low cost of the black-and-white reproduction technique. These tones consist of groups of dots, dashes and stipples. They are either bonded to a self-adhesive carrier sheet which is cut up and applied to artwork or they may be applied using the dry-transfer principle. In most cases, self-adhesive toning is easier and quicker than the dry-transfer type as far as graphs, diagrams and charts are concerned. Self-adhesive tone sheets should be of the "low tack" variety — they should not stick so firmly to the paper surface as to be difficult to remove or replace; the best of these is sold under the trade name of Zipatone. High tack sheets are difficult to handle, and may accidentally remove ink lines. Corrections can be made by an opaque white paint such as Tipp-Ex fluid, which is so indispensable to typists.

Lettering should be done directly onto the drawing or print (such as by a dry transfer) and not stuck on, for even if the paper matches exactly, the edges will show. If the author is not highly skilled at lettering, he should indicate the appropriate positions of his labels on a topsheet of tracing paper, so that the publisher's artist can make the finished labels on the drawing or print.

Halftone Illustrations

Halftone illustrations include photographs, radiographs and wash drawings. Journals which do not use high-quality paper cannot reproduce these well, so an author should examine the journal to which he intends to submit a paper and discuss publication with the editor before deciding whether to include halftones. They are also more expensive to reproduce than line drawings. The ideal illustration for publication contains a full range of tones from white to black with sharp gradations.

Colour Reproduction

The expense of coloured illustrations is such that they should be considered only when author and publisher agree about their use or if the author is able to cover the cost. Much skill is needed for good colour reproduction and the author should bear in mind that a poor colour illustration is worse than a good black and white one. The use of two colours, rather than a wide range, is simpler and cheaper.

Lettering

The study of lettering, especially its decorative quality, has occupied man from his earliest days. Here it is considered only from the functional aspects. Lower case serif styles, apart from looking better, often give a more familiar shape to a word; for one is accustomed to these, as here, in daily newspapers and elsewhere. Too many capitals may be difficult to read. Italics have a more pleasant appearance and are easier to read when lettering has to run vertically, as may be the case on the vertical axis of a graph.

Skill in good lettering depends partly on spacing letters so that the area between each is approximately equal. When writing from a typewriter is compared with print, it will be seen that the latter is better spaced. Each letter of a typewriter has to fill the same area so that w's are compressed and the i's have space around them. In lettering done by hand, by stencilling, by printing, by adhesive letters or by transfers, each space between the letter should be appropriate, and letters themselves should take up the area that their individual shape justifies. Graph paper is a useful background for drawing letters and it should be blue or grey, for the grid lines can be excluded when it is photographed. Words are easier to read if letters are too close rather than too far apart.

For size of lettering, the writer should look at a copy of the journal which he is hoping to favour with his article, and see by how much illustrations will be reduced (as by one half). The size of type of the page can be measured and multiplied (such as twice) to the same scale as the drawing. A safe guide is to make the original lettering 4 mm high, as the minimum legible size for print is 1 mm. The policy of some journals is that lettering of illustrations such as graphs should be left to the printer. It is then only necessary to insert guide lettering in soft pencil.

Graphs

The purpose of a lined graph is to give an immediate picture of trends or changing values. No more than three or four curves should appear in one illustration; coordinates should be spaced widely, and interspaced or unrelated curves avoided. The components of any lined graph are discussed in order of importance below.

Curves: Each curve can be distinguished by a distinctive line form, such as full lines(_____), pecked lines (---------) or dotted lines (.............) (Fig. 6.8). Different symbols can be used for experimental points, the usual ones being: ○ , △ , □ , ● , ▲ and ■ .

Open symbols are generally preferred and geometrical forms print better. Solid symbols can be used for emphasis.

If neither method is used, a brief description can be written alongside each curve. If the description is likely to be long, it is preferable to identify each curve with a number or letter and explain these in the

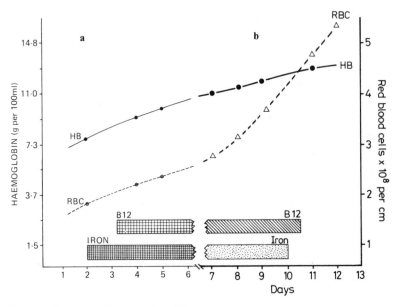

Fig. 6.8. Graph: **a** badly drawn, **b** well drawn.

legend. Flexible rulers or French curves are invaluable for drawing smooth curves.

Axes (coordinates): The vertical and horizontal axes (y and x axes) should be in dark heavy lines, though less thick than the curves; usually the whole is boxed. A horizontal rather than a vertical rectangle aids the printer and should be used when possible.

Axes (captions): Each axis must be labelled clearly with the quantity and units used for measuring, as well as their names. Lettering should preferably be parallel to the base line for ease of reading, but this is usually impossible for the vertical axis.

Grid markings: It is rarely necessary for the reader to be able to make or check computations from line illustrations, so that complete rulings are not necessary. Scale values can, however, be shown by short grid marks (thin line) placed on each axis at suitable intervals; each can be labelled, or just alternate ones, depending on the space available. Scale values should be planned carefully before starting to draw graphs, to avoid the curves being crowded into a single area of the graph (Fig. 6.9); it must reach across the entire illustration. The scale need not start at zero but a

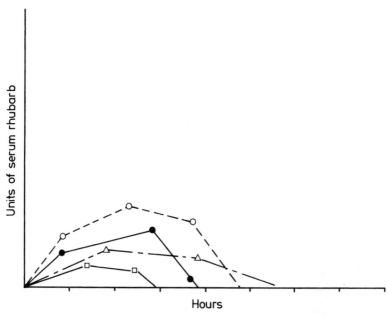

Fig. 6.9. Crowded curves to a graph.

true visual impression must be given and the exaggeration of a faulty scale avoided.

Choice of graph paper is important. Pale blue or grey should be used, and other colours are best avoided.

Shadings can be applied to graphs with patterns of dots, lines, stippling or cross-hatching, but hatching must be applied very carefully, for unevenness causes a patchy appearance and light reflections when photographed.

Bar charts and pie diagrams show at a glance what is incomprehensible in a table of figures, but for accuracy a table is superior to both.

Other Forms of Illustration

Pictorial charts can be constructed by using rows of pictorial symbols (see p. 141) instead of the bars of a bar chart, or a number of objects may be grouped together to illustrate an idea. Perspective diagrams, usually three-dimensional histograms (Fig. 6.10), can relate three or more sets of facts, although care must be taken that they do not mislead or exaggerate.

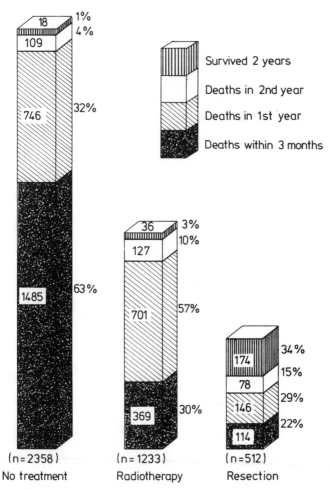

Fig. 6.10. A three-dimensional histogram.

Reproduction of Radiographs

Photographs of X-rays are probably the most difficult form of illustration to reproduce well, because they have to be reproduced from the full-size radiograph to a picture only several centimetres in size and suffer badly as a result of the poor quality of the paper often used for journals. Interpretation of radiographs may be assisted by a simple line drawing as a guide beside it.

Cropping Photographs

When a radiograph is photographed, unnecessary data such as initials, dates, file numbers and so on should be eliminated and the area of principal interest arranged as near to the centre as possible. Cropping away distracting or irrelevant features emphasises the points of the picture and allows a greater size of important aspects. The author leaves actual trimming to the editor so that cropping can be done according to the plan of a particular page. However, he should indicate how he wishes them to be cropped, either by pencil marks in a margin or by tracing on a transparent overlay; the latter must be done without injuring the print.

Photographs of Pathological Specimens and Microscopical Sections

Pathological specimens should be photographed with a centimetre rule alongside to indicate size. Interpretation is often aided by arrows or other suitable markers on the photograph itself. The commonest mistake is that markers are too small when the photograph is reduced for printing. A blue background is often preferable, and bleached specimens can be made presentable by correct choice of emulsions.

Successful photographs of microscopical sections depend as much on contrast as on clear detail. If the original section is not stained satisfactorily, a new section should be cut from the tissue block and stained suitably. Overstaining should be avoided. The optimum magnification which shows the desired characteristic should be used. Very high power may be difficult technically. Opinion differs as to whether to include the exact power of enlargement in the legend, as size changes in publication, but the usual practice is to give the power of the original magnification. The legend should also state the type of stain.

Preparation of Illustrations

An illustration, except a photograph, should have a wide margin, 2.5 cm (1 inch) or more, for handling and for the editor to give instructions to the engraver or to indicate crop marks. The figure itself should be about one and a half times or twice the size of the finished illustration, for it is preferable for the printer to reduce rather than enlarge. A large illustration should be photographed and never sent rolled by post. Photographs must be printed on glossy paper and be unmounted. Each illustration, tables excluded, should be numbered consecutively in Arabic (5) and not Roman (V) numerals. The word figure is set in type, so neither it nor the figure legend should form part of the illustration itself. On the back of each figure, there should be written in *soft pencil* (4B) the word TOP, the author's name and the number of the figure.

It is most important that no mistake is made in any part of the illustration. Although errors in the text can usually be corrected without much labour or expense, this is not so with illustrations and the writer may be expected to meet the cost if the fault lies with him.

Packing and Shipping

Some photographs and drawings are ruined in the post. Three disasters may befall a flat parcel: it may be bent in two to pass through a letterbox, it may be dropped and land on one corner, which breaks, or it may be lost — so keep some spare originals. Photographs must be parcelled flat between oversized pieces of cardboard and never rolled or folded; the parcel labelled "Do Not Bend" should be stiff enough to prevent it being folded, and the corners well padded. Commercial mailers are available. A cracked print is ruined and cannot be retouched.

Borrowing Original Illustrations

If one wishes to use illustrations already published, permission must be obtained from the publisher (not the author) of the book or journal in which they appear. It is a courtesy and often a condition of the loan that reference is made to the author when the picture is used. Permission should, whenever possible, also be obtained from patients who appear in illustrations in a book or journal, even if their eyes are masked. If the identity is neither concealed nor permission for publication obtained, a medico-legal problem could ensue and the author be prosecuted because of lack of confidentiality.

Criteria for Judging Illustrations

The American Medical Association Scientific Publications Division (1964) judges illustrations by the following criteria:

1. *Aptness*: Does the figure truly illustrate, or is it merely a space-filler?

2. *Accuracy*: Are there contradictions between data in the figure and data in the text? Does terminology (and spelling) conform to terminology in the text?

3. *Composition*: Is the overall appearance pleasing? Too crowded? Too bare?

4. *Contrast*: Is there enough contrast between greys, blacks and whites? In the case of photographs, and especially high power photomicrographs, is the definition sharp? In the case of graphs, are the lines and lettering clear and sharp and of a uniform degree of blackness?

5. *Clarity*: Is the figure understandable? Will it require more than a moderate degree of effort on the part of the reader? Are markers needed? If used, can they be seen?

References

AMA Scientific Publications Division (1964) Advice to authors: Guide to preparation of manuscript submitted to the Journal of the AMA and the AMA Specialty Journals. Chicago AMA

Hawkins CF, Dee TF (1973) The department of medical illustration: use and abuse. Med Biol (Ill) 23:74–77

Reynolds L, Simmonds D (1981) Presentation of data in science. Martinus Nijhoff, The Hague

7. A Guide to Statistical Methods

Denis M. Burley

*No human investigation can be called true science
without passing through mathematical tests.*

Leonardo da Vinci (1452–1519)
(in Treatise on Painting, Chap. 1)

As scientists we all have beliefs and the purpose of the scientific experiment is to test those beliefs. Yet medical history is littered with untested beliefs acted upon for decades or even centuries until the application of scientific method has led to their being discarded, often with great reluctance. These might merely concern the theory of medicine or, more importantly, they might concern patients; for example, numerous futile operations were done to remove healthy organs of patients — tonsils, gall-bladders and colons — because of the untested and unproved hypothesis of focal sepsis. A scientific approach is more humane and careful clinical trials prevent useless and dangerous drugs being inflicted upon the public.

Earlier this century injections of gold were thought to benefit patients with tuberculosis. How did this belief arise? Perhaps somebody treated a patient suffering from tuberculosis with gold and they got better. Everytime a new patient treated with gold got better the belief was reinforced, and tended to lead to suppression of contrary data. Since the natural history of untreated tuberculosis leads to recovery in some patients and to death in others, chance results could easily lead to false conclusions about the efficacy of treatment. This is the problem with all therapy: real effects, whether beneficial or harmful, may be obscured and chance happenings may lead to false conclusions.

The purpose of a properly designed medical experiment is to eliminate the effects of belief (bias) and the object of statistics is to disentangle the effects of chance from the true but unknown effects of treatment. The proper application of statistics to medicine is of relatively recent origin but this is not so in many other scientific disciplines. A statistician should be a member of, or available for consultation for, any scientific team, his function being to advise on the method of collecting, processing, analysing and interpreting numerical data. However, statistical methods can never *prove* anything and the answer always comes out as a *probability*; the same applies to assessing results by intuition, except that the probability is not calculated but guessed.

Collecting Data

Before results can be analysed, the data must be collected and this means making measurements of one sort or another. This poses several subsidiary questions:

● What measurements?
● Are the measurements valid?
● Has bias been eliminated?
● Have the observations been recorded and transcribed correctly?

What Measurements?

There are essentially three types of measurement:

1. *Interval (numerical):* This records quantitative data and represents the highest level of measurement. Examples are weighing an object on a balance, using a ruler or blood pressure machine, and levels of biochemical substances in blood or urine.

2. *Ordinal (ranked):* This term is used for the recording of semi-quantitative data or when responses are ranked in order — best result . . . worst result.

3. *Nominal (classified):* Each category or class must be well defined, exclusive (no observation may belong to more than one category) and exhaustive, meaning that all observations must belong to one of the categories. This is often difficult in clinical medicine but a simple example is where an outcome is recorded such as "alive" or "dead", "asleep" or "awake".

It is important to define the type of measurement since different statistical methods have to be applied to each of the above. There is, however, often overlap in the forms of measurement. For example, at necropsy the spleens of 100 patients may be weighed in grams and the interval scale used; but later the ordinal one may be preferred where spleens are specified as very large, large, average or small. Similarly, nominal data may be partially ordered since categories of response can in themselves have a rank order — excellent, good, fair, poor, very poor — although it may be difficult to say that the step from poor to fair is the same interval as the step from fair to good.

Are the Measurements Valid?

A ruler is a valid measure of height and an accurate pair of scales a valid measurement of weight. But does a cheese grater strapped to the arm under a blood pressure cuff give a valid measurement of pain intensity as the mercury column rises, and would it be right to describe it as a hundred millimetres of pain if that is when the subject begs you to stop doing it? Some measuring instruments are like this and it must be considered whether such measurements can be extrapolated to headache, or abdominal pain after operation, as some people might wish to do when they perform a clinical trial of an analgesic drug. In medicine, there is often no clear dividing line.

Has Bias Been Eliminated?

It is easier to round up or round down blood pressure recordings and if a drug that you favour is being given, you might be tempted to round down rather than round up. This type of bias is eliminated in two ways: first by ensuring that at least the observer is unaware which treatment the patient is receiving and secondly by using instruments which do not disclose the true reading until after it has been made. In research on blood pressure, this can be done by the use of a Hawksley Random Zero machine or the more sophisticated though less portable London School of Hygiene machine.

Have the Observations Been Recorded and Transcribed Correctly?

Figures are often recorded incorrectly and different observers can disagree substantially about measurements. It is therefore important to have some knowledge of both inter- and intra-observer error. Most data from record cards or sheets are nowadays transcribed to punch cards (Chap. 2) or computers and their floppy disc storage facilities. Data must be transcribed correctly and the more transcribing that is done, the greater the number of possible errors.

Choosing Individuals to Be Studied

In most research projects it is impossible or impractical to study the effect of treatment on all patients available who might be suffering from a given condition. The total number is referred to statistically as the "population" and the group chosen for study "the sample". It follows that the more representative the sample is of the total population, the more applicable will be the results to that population.

The study of a sample will save time, money and effort; also, since the number of people making the observations will be less, it will be easier to find good specialists and to train them adequately, and the methodology can be more tightly controlled as fewer research instruments will be needed — so their performance can be constantly verified. The disadvantage is the problem of sampling errors, so that the sample may not represent the population itself. This can be reduced by simply increasing the size of the sample and it can be quantified by means of a statistical constant called the standard error (see later).

When a sample is not representative of its population, it is known as a "selected sample". By definition a selected sample cannot be used to draw conclusions about a population, unless it is known fairly precisely in what way the sample differs. There are three ways in which samples may become selected:

● Instances where the sample is taken from a sector of a population with the erroneous belief that this sector forms the whole population.

● Cases where individuals are chosen by a method other than random sampling, for choosing individuals by a random procedure is the only advisable method for providing samples.

● Cases where the sample is chosen correctly but circumstances make it impossible to obtain information from the individuals under study. This happens, for example, when doing surveys by post, where only the people interested in the subject being researched will answer. These people usually have characteristics that are quite different from the rest of the population, and omission of those not replying to any questionnaire will produce wrong conclusions.

Getting the Numbers Right

Clinical trials are usually simple comparisons between two randomised groups, and the number of patients entered into a trial is nearly always determined in advance — and clinical objectives are seldom taken into account when the size of the sample is chosen. Hence the numbers are usually estimated by the length of time or amount of money available, or even by choosing some arbitrarily "round" number. Altman (1983) pointed out that recent reviews of general medical publications and of clinical trials in particular have shown that many studies are too small to have any reasonable chance of detecting clinical benefit of the treatment under investigation and he gives guidelines for getting the numbers right:

● The usual method by which the size of the sample is determined is closely related to significance testing. The object of this is to reduce to an acceptable level the risk of obtaining a misleading result by making statistical significance and clinical importance coincide as nearly as possible.

● The physician should specify either the smallest benefit of the new treatment that would be considered to be of clinical importance or the smallest benefit that it would be important not to miss.

● For trials where the measure is qualitative (or categorical) — improved or not improved, survived or died — an estimate is needed of the proportion with that outcome (such as the death rate) that may be expected in one group, usually the control.

● If the measured outcome is a continuous variable such as the blood pressure, an estimate is needed of the standard deviation (SD) of this. These estimates have to be sought from previous studies or from a pilot study, and allowance has to be made for the fact that participants in the trial are often a highly selected group.

● The researchers must then decide with what probability (known as power) they would wish to obtain a statistically significant result if the benefit of the treatment were exactly equal to the minimum important difference, and they must also specify the significance level, which is usually set at 5% (see later).

If too few patients are used, important therapeutic benefits may not be detected or false-positive findings may be reported, a possibility enhanced by the likely publication being biased in favour of a "significant" result. Unfortunately the continuing uncertainty about various forms of therapy is usually due to the size of the original clinical trials being too small. Large numbers of patients are needed when small differences in response to a drug are expected or when the natural history of the disease varies greatly; an example of this is the use of penicillamine in rheumatoid arthritis, and this type of trial usually has to be done on a multicentre basis. The best way to ensure that numbers in any clinical trial are satisfactory is, of course, to get the expert advice of a statistician.

Definition of Statistical Terms

Every speciality has its jargon and statistics is no exception. The importance of statistical tests cannot be appreciated unless the meaning of terms is understood.

Average is a vague term and when applied to salaries may do little justice to the worker with a low salary (Fig. 7.1). This lay average is

£45,000

£15,000

£10,000

 ⇐ **Arithmetical average**

£5,700

£5,000

£3,700

 ⇐ **Median** $\left(\begin{array}{l}\text{the one in the middle}\\ \text{12 above him, 12 below}\end{array}\right)$

£3,000

 ⇐ **Mode**
$\left(\begin{array}{l}\text{occurs most}\\ \text{frequently}\end{array}\right)$

£2,000

Fig. 7.1. The term average (mean) does little justice to the worker with a low salary. Mode shows what occurs most frequently.

correctly described as the *mean* and is calculated by dividing the total by the number of observations. The *median* divides the curve into equal parts (Fig. 7.2) and the *mode* shows what occurs most frequently and, in the curve, is the frequency density at its maximum. All of these — mean, median and mode — coincide on a curve with a perfectly symmetrical distribution (Fig. 7.3). Sometimes the sides of the curve may not come down fairly sharply as in a bell but tail off as, for example, may happen with certain biochemical estimations of the constituents of blood.

Frequency distributions are tables or histograms constructed from a series of records of individuals — whatever the characteristics measured — to show the frequency with which these occur. With discrete events such as the occurrence of heads or tails on frequent tossing of a coin histograms can be drawn, producing what is known as the *binomial distribution*. Figure 7.4 shows the distribution of events with eight tosses

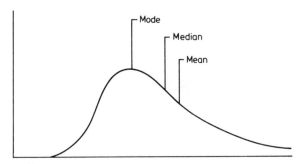

Fig. 7.2. Curve of frequency density to illustrate mean, median and mode.

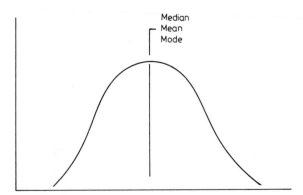

Fig. 7.3. As the curve is perfectly symmetrical, the mean, median and mode coincide (normal, Gaussian, parametric, unimodal).

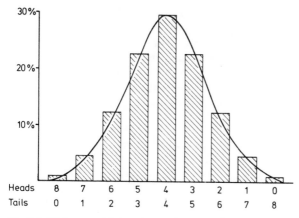

Fig. 7.4. Histogram with superimposed curve to show a frequency distribution.

of a coin, four heads and four tails being the commonest. A curve of sorts can be superimposed. However, if a large number of measurements is available, such as the height of 200 people attending a lecture, then it should be possible to describe a normal or *Gaussian distribution* — a mathematical definition given by Carl Gauss, a German mathematician, when he was 17 years old. This distribution has interesting properties and from it the standard deviation can be calculated as an estimate of the variability of any characteristic under study.

The standard deviation (SD) is located on the curve at the point where it changes from concave to convex; approximately 68% of all observations will lie within this segment (Fig. 7.5). Furthermore if one

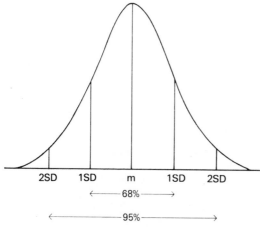

Fig. 7.5. Curve to illustrate standard deviation (SD).

measures off twice the distance, approximately 95% of all observations will lie within the enlarged segment. These intervals are known respectively as 1 and 2 standard deviations. Since the segment covering 2 standard deviations embraces 95% of the observations it follows that the remaining 5% are outside these limits and have a 5% probability of occurrence ($P = 0.05$). However, the standard deviation can be calculated from the observations and the steps are as follows:

1. First list the observations and calculate the mean.

2. Alongside the listed observations write the difference between each value in turn and the mean.

3. These figures are now squared and added up, producing *the sum of squares*.

4. This sum of squares is divided by one less than the number of observations to produce the mean sum of squares or *variance*.

5. By taking the square root of the variance one obtains the *standard deviation*, which can lie on either side of the mean.

Calculations using the height of ten subjects for standard deviation are shown in Table 7.1. The standard deviation is usually shown as mean ± 2 SD as follows:

Table 7.1 Calculations using the height of ten subjects for determining the standard deviation

Height (in.) x	Difference from mean $(x - \bar{x})$	Square $(x - \bar{x})^2$
68	0	0
71	3	9
66	-2	4
60	8	64
67	-1	1
65	-3	9
75	7	49
70	2	4
68	0	0
70	2	4
680		144 = sum of squares $\Sigma (x - \bar{x})^2$

Mean $(\bar{x}) = \dfrac{680}{10}$

$= 68$ in.

$\dfrac{144}{9} = 16 =$ variance $\dfrac{\Sigma(x - \bar{x})^2}{n - 1}$

$\sqrt{16} = 4 =$ standard deviation

$$SD = \sqrt{\Sigma \frac{(x - x)^2}{n - 1}}$$

Mean = 68 in.
SD = 4 in.
Therefore 68 ± 8 is mean ± 2SD.

This mean, and the scatter of values around it as described by two standard deviations, is a much better way of expressing the results than just giving the range of values. Also the two values which describe the limits of two standard deviations in either direction from the mean are 95% probability limits. Normal values for the laboratory data are commonly expressed in this way. In clinical pharmacology blood levels of drugs from limited numbers of subjects should also show the standard deviation to give the best idea of the total scatter of results. The number of estimations should also be given as, for example, for 20 estimations of the serum protein: serum protein 6.7 ± 1.7 g/100 ml (20).

The standard error (of the mean) is a value which is smaller than the standard deviation and does not give a measure of the scatter of individual results but only the likely accuracy of the *mean* value. This point is important when constructing curves from a limited number of observations since the use of the standard error may give a false picture of the reliability of the curve. If one took repeated samples of ten people and measured height, the means would differ and would also be seen to be distributed around an average mean, or population mean if the number of samples was large enough. Ninety-five per cent of all sample means lie within two standard errors of the population mean. Hence a set of results may be expressed as mean ± 2SE. The standard error can be calculated by dividing the standard deviation of a set of results by the square root of the number of observations if the numbers are more than 30, i.e. $SE = \dfrac{SD}{\sqrt{n}}$

What Is Statistical Significance?

Statistical significance is a comment on the degree of probability that observed associations of whatever kind may have arisen through chance. Tossing a coin is a good example. If ten tosses are tried, heads may occur eight times, which may be held to prove that pennies come up heads 80% of the time; this is, of course, nonsense, for a different result may occur on the next trial. If however, anyone had the patience to do a thousand tosses, the results would very likely come out as half heads and half tails — which represents the real probability. Only when there is a substantial number of tests is the law of averages a useful description or prediction. Probability varies widely (Fig. 7.6). By convention a probability (P) of findings occurring by chance not more than one time in 20 ($P < 0.05$) or

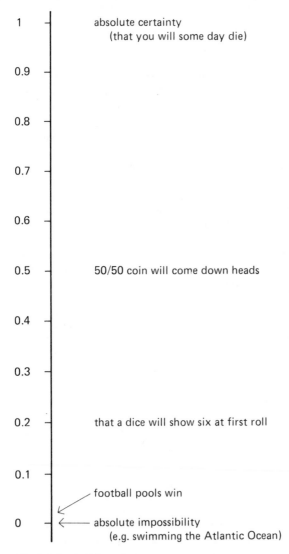

Fig. 7.6. Probability scale.

"significant at the 5% level" is normally accepted as being statistically significant. A probability of findings occurring not more than one time in 100, "significant at the 1% level", or ($P<0.01$) indicates that the findings are highly significant. Statistical significance is, of course, not the same as clinical importance.

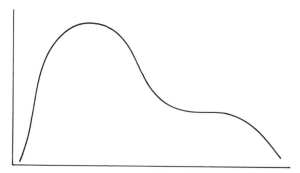

Fig. 7.7. Non-parametric skew distribution.

The term *null hypothesis* is used when the assumption is made, before statistical tests are applied, that there is no difference between two treatments. The statistical test used depends, largely, on the number of observations recorded and the distribution of the results. If the results have a Gaussian (or normal) distribution, familiar parametric tests such as Student's *t*-test can be used. If the distribution (Fig. 7.7) is skewed (non-Gaussian), then transformations will be needed or other statistical methods must be used. Non-parametric tests such as the χ^2 test can be used with any distribution.

Indications for Statistical Tests

How Much Do the Results Vary?

This question is considered by way of numerical calculations. If the frequency distribution is normal or Gaussian, the *standard deviation,* which is more descriptive than range, can be used to study a set of measurements. The *standard error* of the mean allows one to compare two or more sets of measurements. Unfortunately, there is no simple test for skew or non-parametric distributions; sometimes drawing a graph may be helpful.

Are Two Sets of Results "Significantly" Different?

1. Nominal (Classified) Measurements

Most nominal data takes the form of graded categories of response as in Table 7.2. Your eyes will tell you that this analgesic is working but the result could have been due to chance. The 15 "pain worse" patients could have been distributed in this way had we picked them out of a hat, as also could the other categories. A chi square calculation using the formula: $\sum \frac{(O-E)^2}{E}$

will tell you through the use of appropriate tables (see the references) how likely a chance result is (0 stands for the observations actually observed and E for the expected observations had the assignments been random). If the number of observations is small it may be necessary to amalgamate adjacent columns or in a 2×2 contingency table apply Yates' Correction or Fisher's Exact Test. Yates' correction is applied in a fourfold contingency table if the numbers are greater than 40 or between 20 and 40 with no expected frequency less than 5. Fisher's Exact Test is used if the numbers are less than 20 or 20–40 with one or more expected frequencies less than 5.

The McNemar test for paired data: The previous example showed the results of a group comparative study where 50 patients received an analgesic and 50 a placebo. Quite often, however the patients can receive both and make a comparison — a "cross-over comparison". This then provides a pair of responses, one for the analgesic and one for the placebo. This could take the form shown in Table 7.3; of the 50 patients, 10 obtained relief with both analgesic and placebo and 10 had no relief from either. Clearly these 20 do not help us to decide between the two

Table 7.2. A contingency table for nominal data obtained from responses in a drug trial

	No pain	Partly relieved	No relief	Pain worse	Total
Analgesic	20	20	5	5	50
Placebo	5	10	25	10	50

Table 7.3. A "cross-over" comparison providing a pair of responses, one for the analgesic and one for the placebo

	Analgesic Pain relief	No pain relief	
Placebo			
Pain relief	10	5	Total 50
No pain relief	25	10	

148

treatments. Of the other 30, 5 were relieved by placebo but not by the analgesic and 25 by the analgesic but not by the placebo. This difference can be examined by the McNemar test:

$$\frac{(\mid A - D \mid - 1)^2}{A + D}$$ where A and D are the two usable results

$$\frac{(25 - 5 - 1)^2}{25 + 5}$$

$$\frac{19^2}{30} = \frac{361}{30} = 12$$

This result is an χ^2 and can be looked up in the tables under "one degree of freedom", which will tell you that the probability of such a result occurring by chance is less than 1% ($P < 0.01$). For small numbers of comparisons (less than 20) the "sign test" should be used together with the table of binomial frequencies ("c" table).

2. Ordinal (Ranked) Measurements

Wilcoxon's tests for ranked measurements: This is used for ordinal data. The data have both direction and magnitude and are amenable to statistical tests which use the additional data. The magnitude is indicated by the rank order of the results, small differences in treatment response having low ranks and big differences high ranks. If the data are from comparative group trials these may be analysed by the Wilcoxon's sum of ranks test or the Mann-Whitney U test. With paired data from perhaps a cross-over trial the Wilcoxon matched pairs signed rank test can be used.

3. Interval (Numerical) Data

Interval data are analysed by plotting a frequency distribution and using the standard deviation and standard error of the mean. Other tests are as follows:

Student's t-test: The *t*-test was developed by W.S. Gosset, who wrote many papers under the pseudonym "Student". He was not a professional mathematician (his work was, in fact, in the Guinness's brewery in Dublin where he went after studying chemistry and mathematics) but his hobby was statistics and he published his paper in 1908. The *t*-test depends on a comparison of means from a group comparative study, and associates these means with a scatter of the results (SE) using the formula

$$t = \frac{m_1 - m_2}{\sqrt{\dfrac{s^2}{n_1} + \dfrac{s^2}{n_2}}}$$

where m_1 and m_2 are the two sample means and the denominator is the combined estimate of the variance of the means (S^2) divided respectively by the number in each sample, the square root being taken out of the whole. The significance of t can then be looked up in appropriate tables.
Paired t-tests: If the data are paired as in a cross-over study, the mean of the *differences* between the results in each half of the cross-over can be divided by its own standard error, as in the following formula:

$$t = \frac{\text{mean difference}}{\text{SE of the mean}}$$

There are many other statistical tests which depend on the normal distribution, of which the most familiar is Analysis of Variance or the *F*-test.

Sequential Analysis

This is the ultimate in frequent data analysis since results are plotted as they come in. They may be plotted as frequencies on charts of open or closed design, or in the case of interval measurements on a sequential *t*-test chart. Each chart can examine only one comparison but the advantage is that the study is stopped when the plot reaches a chosen level of significance so that it economises in numbers. In medicine this consideration may be important in making ethical decisions about the desirability of continuing a less effective treatment after superiority of the alternative has been shown.

What the Research Worker Can Do Himself

"To learn by doing" is applicable to statistics as with everything else. Any doctor can, with an appropriate calculator (Fig. 7.8) calculate the means and standard deviations, and perform a test of significance on his own data. There is, for example, the electronic calculator with an SD button, and a memory is useful as this can do square roots. Also additional modules can be supplied for Student's *t*-test. A write-out helps, especially for checking that there are no mistakes.

Fig. 7.8. Electronic calculator and module.

The types of error that are common in articles published in journals are shown in Table 7.4. The following are ten important questions which the assessor uses when reviewing a scientific paper and it would be wise for the author to consider these before submitting the article:

1. Have representative samples been taken for the study?
2. Are the groups under study homogeneous (is like being compared with like)?

Table 7.4. Types of statistical error

1. Inadequate description of basic data (range, standard deviation, etc.)
2. Failure of random selection of data
3. Naive belief that data follow Gaussian distribution
4. Disregard for statistical independence
5. Wrong uses of Student's t and χ^2 tests

3. Are there sufficient numbers in the study?
4. Is the data collection complete and accurate?
5. Are the measurements valid and unbiased?
6. Are the measurements nominal, ordinal or interval?
7. Have the measurements been analysed appropriately?
8. Have the results been presented clearly and properly?
9. Has a clear distinction been made between the hypothesis being tested and unexpected findings thrown up in the results?
10. Are the conclusions justified on the basis of the results presented?

Fortunately, Swinscow (1978) writes that complicated statistical methods are rarely necessary for the analysis of medical and many other biological problems. If the research is planned carefully, so that truly comparable, complete and random samples are obtained, then the statistical analysis can be kept as simple as possible. In fact, data that fail to yield a significant result when subjected to simple tests but do so after a refined and complex analysis need to be looked at especially critically.

References

Altman DG (1983) Size of clinical trials. Br Med J 1:1842–1843
Swinscow TDV (1983) Statistics at square one, 8th edn. British Medical Association, London

Further Reading

Gore SM, Altman DG (1982) Statistics in practice (articles from the British Medical Journal). British Medical Association, London

Useful Tables

Clarke CJ, Downie CC (1966) A method for the rapid determination of the number of patients to include in a controlled trial. Lancet II:1357
Diem K, Lenter C (eds) (1973) Documenta Geigy. Scientific tables. Ciba-Geigy, Basle
Fisher RA, Yates F (1970) Statistical tables for biological, agricultural and medical research, 6th edn. Oliver and Boyd, Edinburgh

8. Publication

Jane Smith

The worker who wants his research available to the widest possible audience must seek to have it published. Since original research tends not to be published in books (except for conference proceedings) until it has become integrated into a discipline's body of knowledge, publication for most researchers means publication in a scientific journal.

This chapter deals with choosing a journal, preparing a manuscript for submission, what journals expect of their authors and what they do to their papers once accepted.

Choosing a Journal

Before starting to write his article the researcher should have some idea of whom he is writing for — a small group of fellow experts, for example, or, less likely, the wider scientific community. The prospective audience will govern his choice of journal and the style in which he writes his paper.

Biomedical journals fall into various groups. Among those that publish original research are specialist journals, general medical journals and general scientific journals that publish, among other things, biomedical papers. Other types of journals concentrate on publishing review articles or teaching articles, or they cover up to date work in a newsy fashion; however, a serious scientific report of original research is unlikely to be published in these journals, and it would be a waste of time to send it to them.

The general scientific journals include *Nature, Science, Comptes Rendus de l'Academie des Sciences, Naturwissenschaften* and *Intersciencia*. Their standards are exacting and their rejection rates high. The major general medical journals are the *New England Journal of Medi-*

cine, the *British Medical Journal,* the *Lancet,* the *Journal of the American Medical Association, Presse Mèdicale* and *Deutsche Medizinische Wochenschrift.* All these journals have a bias towards publishing research with a fairly direct relevance to clinical practice. They also include editorials, review articles, news, letters and other material to keep their varied groups of readers entertained and informed. They are weekly journals with large circulations run by full-time editors, and they reject 80%–85% of the papers they receive. The journals of national medical associations (or, in the USA, state medical associations) are also general in content; though they are usually not published as often as the major journals, their circulations are smaller, and their rejection rates are lower.

The third major group of journals is the specialist medical journals, which cover the major specialties, subspecialties and some areas of research. These are usually monthly, bimonthly or quarterly, their delay from acceptance to publication is often several months rather than several weeks, their rejection rates are usually 50%–60% (though some have much higher rates), and their editors are usually full-time clinicians or scientists who edit the journal in their spare time.

Most research articles are likely to be aimed at fellow workers in the same subject and will therefore probably be written for a specialist journal. If the work has demanded collaboration with workers in another specialty and so might interest more than one expert group it may be worth sending it to one of the general journals, particularly if the work has some clinical relevance. Their rejection rates are high, however, and the authors will have to remember that they are writing for a much more disparate readership and that they will probably have to explain more than they would to an audience of fellow experts.

Language may also play a part in selecting a journal. Many researchers have to write articles in languages other than their own if they want to reach a wide international audience. English is the major medical language and the three medical journals with the largest circulations — the *New England Journal of Medicine,* the *Journal of the American Medical Association* and the *British Medical Journal* — are all published in English. Nevertheless, work that has a particularly local interest might be best published in a local scientific journal in the author's own language.

If there is more than one possible journal, factors governing the choice may include area of circulation (primarily European, American or Australasian), the language of the journal, its prestige and reputation and, finally, the preferences of the researcher — he might prefer to submit his article to a journal he likes reading. The instructions to authors section of the journal usually gives a reasonable guide to the sorts of papers that journals will take, and would-be authors must read these instructions (see p.157), but they are much better guided in their choice of journal by close acquaintanceship through regular reading.

Preparing the Manuscript for Submission

The actual writing of the article has been discussed in Chap. 5, but two points are worth emphasising. Firstly, the choice of journal should be made before the paper is written: to write it well the researcher needs to know whom he is writing for. The readers of a general journal will not necessarily share the assumptions common to a group of specialists, recognise the methods by the briefest of names, understand the jargon and translate correctly the abbreviations. If an author always assumed that he was writing for a group of knowledgeable people outside his specialty he would not go far wrong: if he always assumed that he was writing for fellow experts he might fail to get his message across.

Secondly, a paper prepared for delivery at a meeting is, or should be, very different from one written for publication. Delivery at a meeting may be useful preparation for publication because the audience's questions may probe weaknesses in the work or the researcher's account of it and show him where he needs to expand and explain. But the subsequent preparation for publication is more than just changing "slide 1" to "figure 1", expanding the references and putting the typescript in the post with a covering letter.

Speaking demands a different style from writing, with more repetition and emphasis because listeners, unlike readers, cannot go back over a point to absorb it more fully. Points of emphasis may be made into slides for a lecture that would look ridiculous as figures in a paper. Conversely, a table with large amounts of data may be acceptable in a printed article but make an unreadable slide during a lecture (Lock 1977; Hawkins 1967).

If the paper is intended for a journal published in a language other than the author's own and which he has reasonable command of, he should write the manuscript in that language. This usually produces a better result than having the article translated after it has been written. If possible the final version should be checked by a native speaker, preferably someone familiar with the subject. Some journals arrange their own language checking. For example, some Scandinavian journals that publish in English use British scientists as language referees; after assessing the scientific aspects of a paper and deciding that it is acceptable they send it to the language referee, who will, if necessary, rewrite it to improve the language.

Duplicate Publication

A paper should never be sent to more than one journal at the same time. Editors and their referees invest much time and energy in reading papers, assessing their suitability for publication and making suggestions for improvements. Editors do so on the assumption that the decision whether to publish or not is in their hands and not likely to be taken from them by another journal. To mislead them by submitting a paper to more than one journal simultaneously is wrong. If the first journal rejects the paper then, of course, it may be submitted to another.

In general, journal editors do not want to publish material that has already appeared in print. This is not only because they are jealous of their journal's reputation for publishing original material but also, and more importantly, because the scientific literature is large enough already without being cluttered with duplicate material. Other researchers are not well served when searching among published reports to find details of the same work under different guises. This restriction has two main consequences.

Firstly, researchers should resist the urge to squeeze as many papers as possible out of a piece of work. Writing two different versions of an article, one for a specialist audience and another for a general audience, and sending them to two separate journals is usually unethical. Adding a few more rats or a few more patients or even a few more authors to a paper already published and submitting it as further work is also dishonest unless there are special reasons — for example, the results with the new rats or patients (or authors) are radically different from the original findings.

Secondly, if there is any possibility of duplicative publication or the author is in any doubt about it, he should draw it to the editor's attention when he submits his paper. This is a requirement of the Vancouver style (see p.157), which states that copies of any possibly duplicative work should be submitted with the manuscript. For example, a researcher may well have presented his work first at a meeting and only later written it up for publication. In practice most editors will not consider that this prevents them from publishing the paper, even if the delivered paper is due to appear in conference proceedings, but the author should always tell the editor, so that the editor may judge for himself.

Some minority language national medical journals are prepared to publish shortened versions of work that may already have appeared in one of the major medical journals in English. For example, several Scandinavian journals will publish shortened versions of reports from Scandinavian authors that have appeared in, say, the *New England Journal of Medicine*. This enables the author's countrymen to see the work, and it is always accompanied by a reference to the full version, so as not to confuse readers or the indexing agencies.

Instructions to Authors

Journals are looking for well written papers reporting original, well thought out and well analysed research. They want a full account of the methods (so that someone else could do it too), including the statistical analysis; a clear exposition of the findings, with raw data and not just percentages; and lucid speculation about their implications. They would also like the paper to be neatly organised and typed, with clearly drawn diagrams and tables. They may or may not spell out all these requirements in their instructions to authors.

Researchers must read a journal's instructions to authors — preferably before starting to write but certainly before typing up the final version. The instructions to authors, or an abbreviated version of them (Table 8.1), are usually printed prominently in each issue of a journal, often inside the front cover. The instructions may describe the scope of the journal, the sorts of papers it will consider and how it operates its refereeing system. They may also state the requirements for ethical approval of studies in human subjects and the need for informed consent. They will definitely state how many copies should be submitted and how the references should be laid out and include guidance on nomenclature and units of measurements.

The instructions to a biomedical journal may also say that the journal has agreed to accept papers prepared in accordance with the Vancouver style — "Uniform requirements for the submission of manuscripts to biomedical journals" (International Committee of Medical Journal Editors 1982). The Vancouver style, so called because it was drawn up by a group of medical editors meeting in Vancouver, is a set of standard instructions to authors, and over 200 biomedical journals have now agreed to accept the style. This means that if an author follows the instructions of the style those journals will consider his paper for publication without sending it back to him because it does not conform to their own requirements. If the paper is accepted and the journal's publication style differs from that of the Vancouver style the journal itself will make the changes. The style has had the largest impact on the format of references. Indeed, it came about because authors (and their secretaries) complained that journals all had different styles for their references, which necessitated retyping them every time a paper was rejected by one journal and the author wanted to submit it to another.

The Vancouver style uses the numbering system of references. Each reference is given a number according to the order in which it first appears in the text. The reference in the text is indicated by the number, often set superior to the line (like this: [1-4]). The format for the references that the Vancouver style uses is based on that used by the National Library of Medicine in *Index Medicus,* and the first four references would appear in this list as follows:

Table 8.1. Abbreviated instructions to authors from the *British Medical Journal*. Reproduced by permission of the *BMJ*

Instructions to authors

The BMJ has agreed to accept manuscripts in accordance with the Vancouver style (BMJ, 12 June, p 1766) and will consider any paper that conforms to the style. More detailed and specific instructions are given below.

The following include the minimum requirements for manuscripts submitted for publication.

A stamped addressed envelope or an international reply coupon *must* accompany the manuscript if acknowledgement of receipt is desired.

Papers will normally be refereed and may be statistically assessed before acceptance.

(1) Original articles and those submitted for the Practice Observed and Medical Practice sections are normally up to 2000 words long; Short Reports should have no more than 600 words (with one table or figure and up to five references) and letters normally no more than 400 (with up to 10 references). Contributions for the Personal View and Materia Non Medica columns should contain up to 1150 and 400 words respectively.

(2) Authors should give their names and initials, their posts at the time they did the work, and not more than two degrees or diplomas. Each author must sign his consent to publication, and the paper will be assumed to be submitted exclusively to the *BMJ* unless the contrary is stated.

(3) Three copies should be submitted. Two will be returned if the manuscript is rejected.

(4) Typing should be on one side of the paper, with double spacing between the lines and 5 cm margins at the top and left hand side of the sheet.

(5) Abstracts should accompany all original articles. They should be no longer than 150 words and should set out what was done and the principal findings and their implications in terms that will be understood by clinicians in other disciplines.

(6) SI units are used for scientific measurements. In the text they should be followed by traditional units in parentheses. In tables and illustrations values are given only in SI units, but a conversion factor must be supplied.

(7) References must be in the Vancouver style and their accuracy checked before submission. References should be numbered in the order in which they appear in the text. Each reference should include the names and initials of each author (or, if more than six, the first three followed by *et al*), the title of the article, the title of the journal (abbreviated according to the style of *Index Medicus*), the year, the volume, and first and last page numbers. Titles of books should be followed by the place of publication, the publisher, and the year. "Unpublished observations" may not be used as references but may be cited only in the text.

(8) Letters to the editor submitted for publication must be signed personally by all authors.

(9) The editor reserves the customary right to style and if necessary shorten material accepted for publication and to determine the priority and time of publication.

(10) Detailed instructions are given in the *BMJ* of 7 January 1984, p 6.

[1] Lygidakis NJ. Potential hazards of intraoperative cholangiography in patients with infected bile. *Gut* 1982; 23:1015-8.

[2] Gowers E. *The complete plain words.* London: HMSO, 1973:22-4.

[3] Bloggs L, Sissons S. Hiccupping — I. *Journal of Clinical Curiosities* 1957; 78:111-205.

[4] Bloggs L, Sissons S. Hiccupping - II. *Journal of Clinical Curiosities* 1957; 78:267-98.

The other main method — the Harvard system — is based on a list of references given in alphabetical order; in the text the reference is indicated by the name of the author and the date of the work given in parentheses (Gowers, 1973). Two articles by the same authors in the same year are distinguished by letters (Bloggs and Sissons, 1957a, 1957b). In the list these references might appear as follows:

Bloggs L and Sissons S. (1957a). Hiccupping — I. *Journal of Clinical Curiosities* 78:111-205.

Bloggs L and Sissons S. (1957b). Hiccupping — II. *Journal of Clinical Curiosities* 78:267-98.

Gowers E. (1973). The complete plain words. HMSO, London, pp. 22-24.

Lygidakis NJ. (1982). Potential hazards of intraoperative cholangiography in patients with infected bile. *Gut* 23:1015-8

The major point to remember about references is that they must be retrievable. Therefore personal communications, articles submitted but not yet accepted, and information gleaned at conferences should never be given as full references. If they have to be used they should be cited in the text in parentheses as personal communications, giving the name of the source; unpublished observations; or comments made at a conference, naming the conference. Authors should also restrict themselves to citing key references, and not list all possible references that support a statement.

The fact that a journal does consider papers prepared in the Vancouver format does not absolve the author from reading the journal's own instructions to authors.

A few journals are strict about their instructions and may return a manuscript that does not conform (for example, the references are in the wrong style or too few copies have been sent) before they have even considered it. Others will return wrongly styled references for the author himself to correct if they accept his paper.

Some journals, notably those in the basic sciences, may levy a charge on authors. These take two forms: a handling charge on all submitted manuscripts and page charges, which are levied only on those articles that are accepted and which vary according to the length of the paper.

Both these charges are designed to offset some of the costs of assessing and publishing manuscripts, and basic science journals resort to them because, unlike clinical journals, they are less able to tap sources of finance such as advertising.

Titles, Abstracts and Authors

Titles of articles are important. They must attract the eye of the browsing reader, yet they must be accurate, for they may be all that someone scanning a list of references has to go on. "Why are children admitted to hospital?" is a more tempting title than "Reasons for admission of children to hospital," yet gives the same information on what the paper is about. Some journals also ask authors to provide a separate list of key words. These are terms to describe the concepts discussed in the paper. They should be different from the words used in the title, but together with the title they provide a clear guide to the subject and scope of the paper. They are used by indexing and abstracting agencies.

The abstract of a paper should be a proper précis, summarising exactly what the paper says: giving the reasons for the study, the way it was done, the major findings and the conclusions. It should give hard data and not just abstract generalisations. The abstract may be all that many people will read; or it may be all that other workers have to go on in deciding whether or not to look up the full paper or send for a reprint.

Authorship and the order in which authors are listed are two vexed questions. Ideally, the question of who should be an author should have been decided at the beginning of the writing if not the beginning of the work, but all too often it is a matter of negotiation at the last minute after the paper is written. The person who actually writes the paper presents the least problem; he or she has usually played a major part in doing the work and in many units the convention is to put his or her name first. Likewise, it is a common convention that the head of the department, if he has had some part in the work, should go last. There are no guidelines on the ordering of any remaining authors. But journal editors are becoming increasingly concerned about a too-casual attitude to authorship: authorship granted in return for routine technical help; to a colleague in return for inclusion in his paper; to the chief simply because he is the chief and in return for the prestige his name confers. No one should be named as an author who has not made a substantial contribution to the work. The acid test is the ability to take responsibility for it: if two out of three authors were run over by a bus would the third be able to answer questions and criticisms about the work? If the answer is no, should he really be an author?

It might seem redundant to point out that all authors should know that they are authors, but too many people have sat down to read one of their regular medical journals only to find their own name staring at them from the top of an almost unknown paper. For this reason the Vancouver style requires the corresponding author to state when he submits his paper that all authors have seen and approved the final version. Some journals demand that all authors sign the covering letter. If authors subsequently make substantial changes or revise their paper all of them should see and approve the amended version. Likewise, if an author is later added or removed from the paper his signature must be given.

Authors should also obtain the approval of those people they want to mention in their acknowledgements.

Submitting the Manuscript

Once he has checked the following points the author is ready to send off his manuscript.

Text: The text should be neatly typed with at least double spacing and generous margins. The correct number of copies must be sent.

Tables and illustrations should not be typed or pasted into the body of the text but presented on separate sheets at the end. (This is because printers will set text and tables separately, and illustrations are made by a different process altogether). Tables should be correctly numbered and a reference to each table must be given in the text; they should also be accompanied by their legends. Figures, however, should have their legends typed on a separate sheet. The figures themselves should be identified on the back by the figure number, the authors and the title of the paper. This information should be written lightly with pencil; the firm pressure of a biro may dent the surface of the photograph and ruin it. Photographs should not be attached to the paper with paper clips, as these may also damage them, and if an author wants to indicate part of the photograph with an arrow or some other mark it is best to tape a piece of tracing paper over the photograph and mark the arrow on the tracing paper. The tops of photographs should be indicated and the stains and magnifications of histopathological photographs given in the legends. Photographs of people should have their eyes masked to prevent identification, or the author should include copies of the subject's consent to his or her photograph being used. At the final stage the author should go through the paper, making sure that all numbers given in tables and figures add up, that they agree with the figures in the text and that if he is using percentages he also gives the raw figures.

Copyright: If tables, figures or substantial parts of the text have been borrowed from other published papers or books the author must include copies of permissions given by both author and publisher.

References should be typed in the correct style and checked to make sure that all the information is there. Each reference in the text must be listed at the end, and each reference in the list must be mentioned in the text. A missing or wrong reference is probably the commonest query that journals have to make, even on the best presented manuscripts.

Author's names and addresses: Journals invariably want to print the addresses or institutions of authors, and writing down five authors and three institutions without showing which name belongs to which place is unhelpful. Many journals also want authors' degrees, and if they ask for only two per author there is no point in giving more. It may be appropriate to include an address for reprints, and it should be made clear which author will deal with the proofs.

The paper should be sent to the journal with a brief covering letter, addressed to the editor, explaining why his journal has been chosen. It should be sent in a strong envelope stiffened with cardboard to protect any photographs.

Authors should keep a copy of all the material sent, including illustrations, tables and photographs. The journal will usually acknowledge receipt of the manuscript.

Inside the Office of the Journal

Once a paper arrives in the journal's office the process of consideration begins. Generally a paper will be read first by the editor, one of his assistants or a member of the editorial board, who will then decide whether it should go to a referee and which one. Some journals, usually specialist ones, send nearly all papers to referees, whereas others initially weed out those that are clearly unsuitable. General journals, for example, often receive papers that are clearly too specialist for that journal and will simply return them unrefereed. The number of referees that a paper is sent to also differs between journals — some usually send it to one, others always to two.

The questions that journals ask of their referees differ greatly in scope: some journals may even ask them to comment on and attempt to improve the way the paper is written. But essentially editors want referees to comment on the methods and scientific reliability of the work and on its originality. Referees usually remain anonymous, even if their comments are passed on to the author.

162

Table 8.2. Examples of the types of questions put to the referee of an article

- Does the article contain original work or is it a comprehensive review of an important subject?
- Is it scientifically reliable — including the ethical and statistical aspects?
- Is it suitable for this particular journal?
- Comments on other aspects such as the scientific argument and the English style.

So check that your article fulfils these criteria before submitting it for publication.

Done properly, refereeing is a time consuming task. Journals, and through them authors, rely heavily on the refereeing system (Table 8.2), and editors cannot demand too much speed of their referees, particularly as they are usually not paid. At least a month and possibly longer is therefore likely to elapse before the referee returns the paper and his report to the editor. If the first two referees disagree and the paper has to go to a third or if the paper includes much statistical analysis and is sent also to a statistician more time will elapse. Authors should not be surprised if it is several weeks before they hear from the journal.

The decision comes in one of four forms: outright rejection (which is common), outright acceptance (which is rare), acceptance subject to modification and an offer to reconsider if the authors revise their paper. The decision is made not by the referee but by the editor, and any disagreement must be with the editor. Nevertheless, editors do rely heavily on their referees, and to some extent they rely on feedback from authors to assess their referees. Many journals will automatically send a copy of the referee's comments to the author, whatever the decision (and others will do so on request). If the paper is accepted subject to modification the suggested revisions will probably be those of the referee, and if the decision is to reject, the referee's comments may suggest how the paper could be restructured to make it acceptable (or show why it will never be acceptable).

On being rejected an author will naturally feel aggrieved. But if, after cooler reflection (and, better still, an impartial colleague's opinion), he still thinks that the referee's criticisms were invalid or that he has misunderstood the point (perhaps it was not expressed very clearly?) he should write politely to the editor. He should explain why he disagrees with the referee, perhaps suggest some amendments to make the paper clearer, and ask the editor to reconsider. If the points are reasonable most editors will be happy to do so and will probably send the paper to a further referee. If he wishes, the author may ask the editor not to send the paper to a particular referee if he thinks he may not get a fair hearing.

If the editor offers to consider the paper again after modification, the author has to decide whether he wants to make the changes and try again or simply submit the paper as it is to another journal. An offer of publication subject to modification is, however, a serious offer, so the author should make the modifications promptly and return the amended paper; if it is not resubmitted within 2 or 3 months it may be regarded as a new paper. Suggested modifications usually improve a paper, but if an author disagrees he may either argue the issue with the editor (politely) or withdraw his paper and submit it elsewhere. If he does withdraw it and resubmit it he should remember that in some small areas of research the second journal may well send it to the same referee as the first — and his comments will presumably be the same.

Sometimes an article is rejected because it is unsuitable for the particular journal (Table 8.3), and it can be sent to another. Alternatively, it can be rewritten in another form, such as a short communication for a journal which encourages these, or as a letter. A well written letter is a useful and rapid form of communication. It should be sent to the editor marked 'for publication' and contain not more than 250 words and not more than two or three references. The letter column of a medical journal constitutes one of the most rapid means of publishing current information, and is especially suitable for reporting isolated clinical observations which do not require lengthy comment or excessive documentation. Letters allow writers to exchange opinions with other workers while the subject is still fresh, and those that contain new or unusual facts may be indexed in the *Index Medicus*. However, note that some journals have a policy of publishing only those letters which relate to something that has already appeared in the journal or in the correspondence column.

Once an article has been accepted for publication no changes should be made to it. If an author realises that he has left out something *crucial* or got some figures wrong he should ring up the journal as soon as he discovers it and warn them of the mistake; otherwise (and as well) he should send written details of the amendments. Some journals also allow important supplementary information or further cases to be added to the end of the paper at proof stage.

On acceptance the journal may ask the author to assign copyright to the journal.

Table 8.3. Reasons why an article may be rejected

- The logic or validity of results is doubtful
- The matter is not original and merely repeats work already published
- Unsuitable for the journal
- The article is too long for the information which it contains
- The article is written badly and is difficult to read.

Editing

The journal's editorial staff will edit the paper and prepare it for the printers. Again, the amount of editing a paper gets varies enormously between journals and depends not only on the quality of the paper itself but also on the size and resources of the journal. Small specialist journals with a part-time editor and part-time technical editor/secretary clearly have less opportunity for editing than large journals with full-time staffs. Nevertheless, many part-time editors devote a lot of time to editing papers — with the aim of clarifying the author's message.

All journals will (or should) check grammar, spelling and punctuation, lay out tables and figures, and check the paper for internal consistency — that the figures given in tables match those in the text, that the references are correctly numbered and so on. Journals will also have a policy on nomenclature, the use of units of measurement, and spellings — their *house style* — and preparation for the printer will include putting papers into the house style and marking up the type sizes. Some journals go much further and rewrite fairly extensively. International journals are used to getting papers from authors whose first language is not English, and they will usually spend some time making the language of these papers clearer, so that they can be read easily by their readers, many of whom also do not have English as their first language.

During this stage the editing staff may contact the author to raise questions about missing references or figures that do not add up. These queries should be answered as soon as possible.

Proofs

In the past the author next saw his paper in galley proof. Now some journals will send an edited typescript instead, because any corrections are cheaper and easier to make than they would be in the typeset article. Whether he receives a typescript or a proof, however, the author should read it carefully, sign it and return it promptly.

Proof are not for rewriting, adding material or having second thoughts about the elegance of the style. They are for checking that nothing has been missed out and that the meaning has not been changed in the process of converting the paper into its published form. The author should therefore read the proof twice, once with the original copy to make sure that nothing has been missed out and that all the figures are correct and again on its own to make sure there are no typographical errors. He should check tables and illustrations particularly carefully for these may have been redrawn or relaid out, and he should answer any questions marked on the proof by the editors.

If changes have to be made there are standard proof correction marks (Fig. 8.1) and some journals will send a copy with the proof. The important point to remember is that although the place where the

∧	Correct as margin indicates	≡	Under word means caps
stet	Let it stand	=	Under word small caps
x	Battered letter	—	Under word means Italic
≡	Straighten lines	*rom*	Change to Roman
√√√	Unevenly spaced-line up	*ital*	Change to Italic
No ¶	No paragraph	*bf*	Bold face
out see copy	Omission here	⌐	Comma
¶	Paragraph	;/	Semicolon
trs	Transpose	⊙	Colon
ℒ	Delete as indicated	⊙	Period
ℒ	Delete—close up	?/	Interrogation mark
⊙	Upside down	!/	Exclamation mark
⊂	Close up	/=	Hyphen
#	Insert space	ℒ	Apostrophe
⌣	Push down this space	66/99	Quotation marks
⊔	Indent one em	ℒ	Superior letter or figure
[/]	Move to left/or to right	ℒ	Inferior letter or figure
⌐/⌣	Raise/or lower	[|]	Brackets
////	Hair space letters	(|)	Parenthesis
wf	Wrong font	¹/m	One-em dash
sc	Small capitals	²/m	Two-em dash
Caps	Capitals	*lc*	Lower case
C+sc	Caps—small caps	*or?*	Is this right?

Fig. 8.1. Standard proof correction marks. Note that these may differ slightly elsewhere from the U.K.

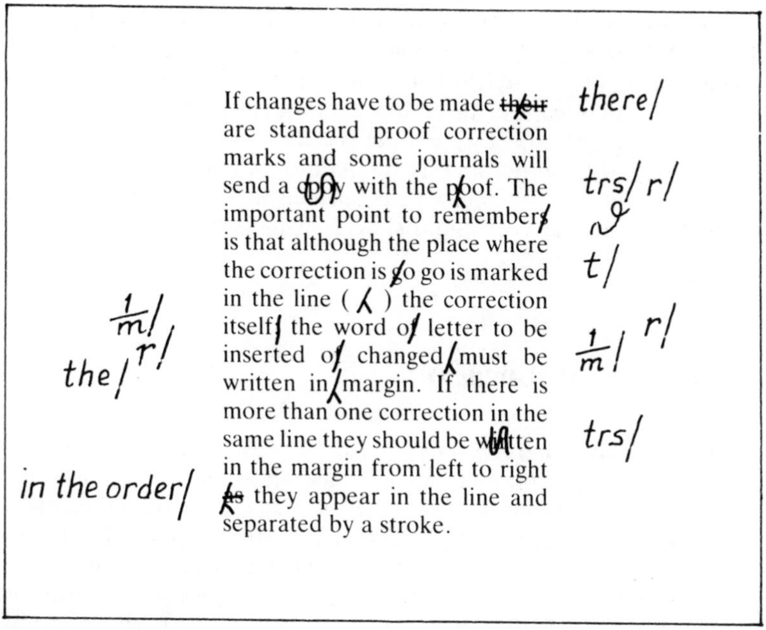

If changes have to be made ~~their~~ are standard proof correction marks and some journals will send a copy with the proof. The important point to remember is that although the place where the correction is go go is marked in the line (ʌ) the correction itself the word or letter to be inserted or changed must be written in margin. If there is more than one correction in the same line they should be written in the margin from left to right as they appear in the line and separated by a stroke.

there/

trs/ r/

t/

m/ r/

trs/

m/ r/

the/ r/

in the order/

Fig. 8.2. Method of correcting proof.

correction is to go is marked in the line (ʌ) the correction itself, the word or letter to be inserted or changed, must be written in the margin (Fig. 8.2). If there is more than one correction in the same line they should be written in the margin from left to right in the order they appear in the line and separated by a stroke. Corrections are put in the margin because the printer will not reread the whole text; he merely looks down the margins and makes corrections only where he sees them. If a word or phrase needs changing, the author should try to replace it with a word or phrase of the same number of characters and spaces, to minimise the amount of resetting that is needed.

If an author notices changes in his wording he should not immediately assume that the editors have got it wrong and change it back but look carefully to see whether the new version is not in fact an improvement. The editors may have picked up ambiguities and rewritten a section to clarify the sense, asking the author to verify it. It is unhelpful merely to reinstate the original wording: that is what caused the problem in the first place, and if the editors in the journal's office are unclear of the meaning the chances are that at least some readers will be too. If the editors have changed the meaning then, of course, the author must correct it and try to write as clearly as he can what he meant. Again, the editors probably got it wrong because it was not completely clear in the first place.

There is no point in changing spellings, the use of capitals or hyphens. They will have been altered to conform with the journal's house style, and a journal's house style is not open to negotiation.

Journals will often say when they want proofs returned by and assume the author's approval if they are not returned in time. It is sensible to keep a copy of the proof and its corrections. A few journals may later send page proofs, so the author can see that his corrections have been made, but no further corrections should be made at this stage.

Waiting for Publication

Authors usually order reprints or offprints when they return their corrected proofs. Some journals give authors some free reprints and allow them to buy more. Their cost depends on the length of the article, the quality of the paper and whether they are offprints or reprints. An offprint is an extra copy of the article made at the same time as the journal is printed — so it will look exactly the same as it did in the journal. A reprint is a copy of the article that is reprinted separately afterwards, often with a different layout. With reprints it may be possible to correct something that was wrong in the original; with offprints it is not.

If the author is lucky enough to have had his paper accepted by one of the large weekly journals it may be a matter of only weeks before he sees it in print. His problem is then to watch anxiously the letter columns to see whether his paper has aroused a hostile response or (possibly worse) no response at all. Most authors, however, will have to wait several months before the paper appears because specialist journals have much longer waiting times and publish less frequently. Authors often complain about the length of time it takes to get their articles published, but the time taken to referee a paper, prepare it for publication and get it into print is small compared with the time it took the author to think about the work, do it, write the paper and make any revisions to it (Roland and Kirkpatrick 1975). And journals need backlogs just as surgeons need waiting lists, so that the editor can put together a balanced journal each issue and have the opportunity of grouping papers on the same topic. In the meantime the author may cite his forthcoming paper as "in press" and start thinking about the next one.

References

Hawkins CF (1967) Speaking and writing in medicine. Charles C. Thomas, Springfield, Ill, pp 3–17

Lock S (1977) Thorne's better medical writing. Pitman Medical, Tunbridge Wells, pp 78–85

Roland CG, Kirkpatrick RA (1975) The lapse between hypothesis and publication in the medical sciences. N Engl J Med 284:1273–1276

International Committee of Medical Journal Editors (1982) Uniform requirements for manuscripts submitted to biomedical journals. Br Med J 284:1766–1770

Appendix A

Suggestions for Those Intending to Present an MD Thesis

The degree of Doctor of Medicine (MD or DM) in the United Kingdom is a higher doctorate which is coveted by medical graduates, being equal in status to doctorates in other university faculties; this contrasts with practice in countries elsewhere in Europe and in the USA, where it is solely a qualifying degree like the MB or BS. A doctorate of philosophy (PhD) is also awarded to medical graduates, though it tends to have a lower status as it is the result of supervised research often obtained at the start of a career. The use of the word philosophy for a science degree is anachronistic: it dates back to the original meaning of philosophy, which covered wisdom and knowledge generally.

The MD thesis is a test of scientific rather than clinical ability and normally provides some contribution to medical knowledge. The most important quality needed for undertaking it is enthusiasm for original work and for studying a subject in depth. It also comes easier to those who have already written articles and received the criticism of editors.

A copy of the regulations for those taking the MD thesis should be obtained from the university and you must read these. Sometimes "notes on the presentation and the binding of theses and reports" are also available. Next go to a medical school library and ask to see the MD theses. Shelves of books bound in the same way will be seen; some MDs may extend to three volumes but others are small. Take some out and look at them and study their format, which is standardised. You will also see that reprints of the author's published work can be included and these are put at the end of the volume. Appendices together with any other material are bound similarly. MD theses have included gramophone records, tapes, a published book and a computer print-out.

The anatomy of an MD thesis is as follows:

Preface: The author states in about 50 words what his object is and the methods used.

Synopsis: A summary of 200 to 500 words describing the contents of the thesis.

Survey of Previous Work: This should be a study in depth of literature concerning the subject. A critical approach, especially of the reliability of previous work, is essential.

Materials and Methods

Results

Discussion

Conclusion

References: Some type of index card system should be used at the start, otherwise much time will be wasted in the final throes chasing up lost references.

Acknowledgements: Mention everyone who has helped, including those in laboratories who have done work not normally part of their routine.

Appendices: Details of special apparatus and so on can be included.

Generally theses are not more than 50 mm thick, and two volumes are made if there are more than 250 pages. Pages must be numbered all the way through, either at the foot of the page or at the top right hand corner. Three copies are usually bound; eventually the top copy is kept in the medical school library, one is customarily left in the department where the work was done and one is kept by the author. Authors should arrange the thesis so that it is easy for an examiner to read — charts, tables and diagrams being close to the relevant text. Abbreviations must not be used unless explained on the first occasion.

Careful thought must be given to the topic, which should be discussed with one's chief and any others who might help. Originality is important. However, an excellent piece of work confirming what is known would also be acceptable. It should represent from 1 to 3 years full-time research. The assessor will want to know how much of the work was done by the author himself and some universities will require a written statement about this. Reprints of previously published work can be used, sometimes being put in a pocket at the end. However, there must be a consistent theme running throughout; a disjointed thesis with no theme will be turned down, so it is no good pinning together a few vaguely related articles. An uncritical approach with a badly argued case must be avoided. Sometimes statistics do not make sense and do not support the argument and this will cause rejection.

The writing must be concise and clear. If you have doubt about this, submit a few pages to someone interested in writing. Many workers tend to be long-winded and make it a burden for the assessor to read. Figures, diagrams, graphs and legends must all be checked; sometimes a figure inadvertently appears upside down or the wrong way round. Other problems include bad typing and spelling mistakes, and inaccurate references; some universities require a signed statement that the author has read all the references to which he refers.

The assessor can recommend (a) that the degree of MD with honours be awarded, (b) that the degree of MD be awarded, (c) that the work is resubmitted after alterations or additions, (d) that an oral examination is held and (e) that the degree of MD is not awarded.

Appendix B

How Best to Use a Dictating Machine

Writing should be postponed until a detailed plan has been made, even as far as outlines of paragraphs and construction of sentences. The first draft is best written or typed by the author himself; then it can be put on tape for the secretary. The dictating machine, when used without the script in mind, is a menace — for it encourages verbosity and a colloquial style. Dictation can drone on endlessly, encouraging those who enjoy the cadence of their own voices. The following guidelines may help to save the time of the secretary and make her job more enjoyable.

● Find out the secretary's knowledge of medical words and spell out *slowly* any that she is unlikely to know — and any unusual words or names otherwise.

● Leave out visual material, like letters which she has to reply to, and write down any unusual spellings or names.

● Do not forget to mention punctuation: stops, commas, semicolons, new paragraphs and so on.

● If you have second thoughts about what you have dictated, *erase and start the bit again*. Otherwise she will have to begin the letter or page all over again.

● Tell her whether an article should be typed quickly as a rough draft, or if it is the final draft which must be done perfectly.

● When the article is finished, make sure the secretary keeps the *top copy* and sends copies to all authors or others who may make corrections.

● Using a machine is impersonal, so the personal touch is even more important. Address her by name, for example, "Jane, please look this up" and give her responsibility, perhaps asking her opinion from time to time. Dictating directly to her occasionally is invaluable as it will keep her up to scratch with her shorthand and improve rapport with her.

Appendix C

Examples of Needless Words that Cause Verbosity

One Word Instead of Several

a decreased number of	fewer
a degree of	some
adjacent to	near
aetiological factor	cause
a large number of	many
a large proportion of	much
a majority of	most
an adequate amount of	enough
an increased amount of	more
anterior aspect	front
a number of	several
at a rapid rate	rapidly
at some future time	later
at the present time	now
a variety of	various
be of the same opinion	agree
be in favour of	support
bring about	cause
by means of	by, with
casual factor	cause
cells of the mononuclear type	mononuclears
circular in outline	circular
come to the conclusion	conclude
come to the same conclusion	agree
conflict of opinion	disagreement
decreased in length	shortened
decreased in thickness	thinned
decreased in weight	lighter
decreased in width	narrower
definitely proved	proved
due to the fact that	because
encountered more frequently	commoner
fatal outcome	death
familiarize oneself	study
fewer in number	fewer
fifty per cent	half
focal areas	foci

for the most part	mainly
give an account of	describe
has been engaged in a study of	has studied
has a tendency to	may
I cannot disguise from myself that	
it would appear	apparently
in a large number of cases	often
in a lateral direction	sideways
in a paravertebral position	paravertebral
incline to the view	think
in close proximity to	near
in considerable quantities	abundant
increased in length	lengthened
increased in size	enlarged
increased in weight	heavier
increased in width	widened
inferior extremity	leg
in few instances	seldom
in most cases	usually
in some instances	sometimes
in the absence of	without
in the affirmative	yes
in the event that	if
in the neighbourhood of	near
in the not too distant future	soon
in the order of	about
in the vicinity of	near
is capable of	can
is characterised by	shows
is suggestive of	suggests
it is clear that	clearly
it would appear that	apparently
not in accordance with the facts	false
of a mild nature	mild
of common occurrence	common
of considerable size	large
of long standing	old
of the chronic type	chronic
on a previous occasion	before
on no occasion	never
on numerous occasions	often
on one occasion	once
on two occasions	twice
owing to the fact that	because, as
paediatric age group	children
place a major emphasis on	stress

present only in small numbers	scanty
presents a picture similar to	resembles
prior to	before
quite a large quantity of	much
red in colour	red
serves the function of being	is
subsequent to	after
sufficient number of	enough
superior extremity	arm
the predominant number of	most
the vast majority of	most
to all intents and purposes	virtually
try out	test
two equal halves	halves
unanimity of opinion	agreement
undergo transformation	change
was of the opinion that	believed
what is the explanation of?	why
with regard to	about

Short Phrases for Long

an upper intestinal barium study	a barium meal
on an out-patient basis	as an out-patient
adverse climatic conditions	bad weather
the radiographic cardiovascular silhouette	the heart shadow
worthy of trial	worth trying
the majority of authors	most authors
an excessive amount of	too much
an inadequate amount of	too little
an inch in breadth	in inch broad
in inch in length	an inch long
a small number of	a few
assume the erect position	stand up
assume the recumbant position	lie down
at a distance from	away from
a relationship to	related to
cases of short duration	short cases
commonly occurs	is common
created the possibility	made possible
diversity of opinion	many views

have the appearance of	look like
has a course of long duration	is chronic
in almost all instances	nearly always
it has been reported by Jones	Jones reported
it is generally believed	many think
it is possible that the cause is	the cause may be
occasional cases	some cases
of constant occurrence	always present
of sufficient size	large enough
on account of	because of
personally speaking	I think
the general opinion is	many think
the present author believes	I think

Superfluous Phrases

Unnecessary qualifying words are another source of verbiage. Authors should, whenever possible, take responsibility rather than hiding behind such terms as:

Authorities agree that . . .
It is a well-known fact that . . .
It is recognized that . . .

Similarly, vague introductory statements may kill whole sentences or paragraphs. The following are typical clichés:

A difference of opinion exists regarding . . .
Although certainly not a new finding, it is important to point out that . . .
At the risk of over-simplification . . .
I have no hesitation in saying . . .
It has been demonstrated that if . . .
It has been proposed that . . .
It is interesting to note that . . .
It is the purpose of this paper . . .
It should be emphasized that . . .
One other consideration should be mentioned . . .
Perhaps, at first sight, it may seem likely that . . .
There are relatively few studies reported . . .
Various explanations have been proposed . . .
We are repeatedly reminded of the necessity for consideration of . . .

Appendix D

American and British Usage in Spelling

The main sources of confusion are ae and oe, both of which are usually kept in British use but almost always contracted to an e in American. Differences that are less important include the American -or for -our, f for ph, and the terminals -ter for -tre, or -er for re, and -ize for -ise.

The following lists are not intended to be complete; rather, they provide some examples of American–British equivalents that will serve as guides.

	American	*British*
e for ae	etiology	aetiology
	anemia	anaemia
	anesthetic	anaesthetic
	cecum	caecum
	defecation	defaecation
	diarrhea	diarrhoea
	hematuria	haematuria
	pediatric	paediatric
e for oe	celiac	coeliac
	edema	oedema
	esophagus	oesophagus
Suppression of final al when it follows ic	physiologic	physiological
Omission of silent endings	program	programme
	catalog	catalogue
	gram	gramme
Terminal -er for -re	center	centre
	fiber	fibre
	liter	litre
f for ph	sulfonamide	sulphonamide
	sulfur	sulphur
k for c	leukocyte	leucocyte
Omission of u when combined with o	color	colour
	tumor	tumour
Miscellaneous	inquire	enquire
	artifact	artefact

Appendix E

Abbreviations of Journal Titles

The following are some examples of abbreviations accepted by the International Committee of Medical Journal Editors.[1] The titles of journals with their abbreviation are printed annually in the January issue of *Index Medicus* at the start under "list of the journals indexed". If in doubt, spell it out — in full.

Acta Paediatr Scand
Am Heart J
Am J Med
Ann Intern Med
Ann Rheum Dis
Arch Dermatol
Arch Intern Med
Aust J Derm
Bangladesh Paediatr
Blood
Br Med J
Can Med Assoc J
Dtsch Med Wochenschr
Eur J Clin Invest
Gastroenterology
Gut
JAMA
J Clin Invest
J Fac Med (Baghdad)
J Immunol
J Irish Coll Physicians Surg

J Lab Clin Med
J Med Ethics
J Med Genet
J Nucl Med Technol
Lancet
Malay J Pathol
Med Clin North Am
N Carolina Med J
N Engl J Med
Postgrad Med J
Quart J Med
Radiology
Rev Clin Esp
Rev Med Chil
Revista Microsc Electron
S Afr Med J
Sem Hosp Paris
Sri Lankan Fam Physician
Ugeskr Laeger
World Med J

1. Uniform requirements for manuscripts submitted to biomedical journals. (1982) Br Med J 284:1766–1770

Guide-lines for Putting Up Poster Displays

Poster displays, often part of the programme of a medical meeting, are useful for showing new research; members can question those who man the exhibits. While accuracy is essential, a display should stimulate interest rather than present complete details, so visual attraction is important.

Make sure that you have received details about the stand, such as measurements and method of fixing exhibits. Everything should be at a reasonable eye level.

Main Headings. The poster should be numbered as in the programme. The title must be succinct and to the point, preferably in the smallest space; a long one may not fit on the display panel. Names of authors should be in slightly smaller lettering and their address is important at international meetings.

Then in sequence, usually from left to right, comes Introduction, Aims and Methods, graphs or tables illustrating the Results, and Conclusions; References, about six, are usually appreciated.

Lettering. Must be large enough to allow people to stand well back so as not to block the views of others. Test it from a distance of 4 feet. It should be bold and black. The size of letters will depend on the type of print and background but up to 30 mm can be considered for the title, 20 mm for the names of authors and about 4 mm for the text. Lettering can be made by the electric typewriter with an IBM golf ball head attachment with a bigger typeface (the orator makes capital letters of 4 mm), by stencilling or by dry transfer lettering (e.g. Letraset).

Data. Can be presented in various ways: graphs and histograms, drawings and diagrams, colour prints, X-rays or slides (if equipment available), paintings or even cartoons.

Don't Overcrowd. Simplicity is essential. Too much material is impossible to grasp. Overcrowding is a similar risk as with the railway timetable type of slide. Arrange the material with plenty of space between the exhibits and avoid them being too cramped. Colour can be important, especially if used logically, and helps to entice the viewer.

Method of Arranging Material for a Travelling Exhibit. There are two methods:

1. Each illustration can be put on separate bits of cardboard. This makes the exhibit easily portable in a suitcase and easier to fit in an awkward space on the stand, and may allow a more attractive layout. It needs more time to put up the poster.

2. The illustrated material can be mounted on 'blockboard' or 'heavy duty' card beforehand. This saves time at the meeting but can provide problems. For example, dimensions of the stand may be given wrongly: the measurement for the exhibit may be stated as 6×4ft, but on arrival it may be vertical and not horizontal, so the board cannot be fitted in — or space may be angled or split.

Methods of Fixing. These vary and should be tested beforehand: panel pins, drawing pins or velcrose. Other ways are by Scotch double stick tape, Sellotape, sticky fixers, Bostik, Blu-tack or Pritt buddies (more than one may be needed for each card). It is wise to take scissors, sellotape and extra pins.

At the Meeting. Arrange for authors to be on hand during the poster session to answer questions. Handouts providing details of techniques for those interested or reprints of previous relevant work can be provided.

Index